# *Shadows of His Sacrifice*

By
*Leslie Hardinge*

**TEACH Services, Inc.**
Brushton, New York

Copyright © 1959 Leslie Hardinge
Copyright © 1996 TEACH Services, Inc.

ISBN 1-57258-065-8
Library of Congress Catalog Card No. 95-61887

Illistrations by Harry Baerg

Published by

**TEACH Services, Inc.**
RR 1, Box 182
Brushton, New York 12916

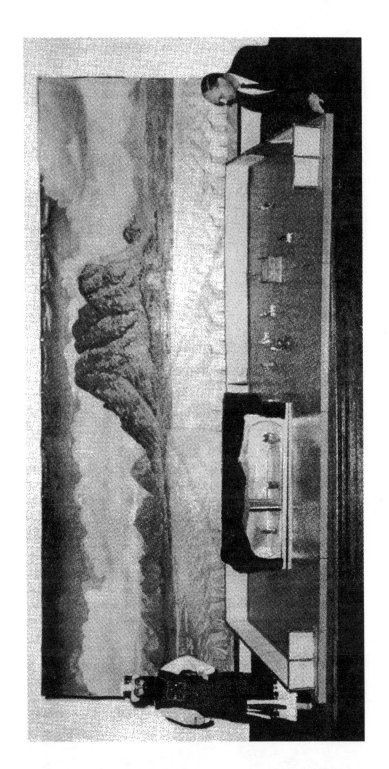

*Model Tabernacle Built to the Scale of $1^1/2$ to the Cubit*
*Photo by Don Roth*

—

# TABLE OF CONTENTS

Introduction........................................ vi

Study I............................................. 1
   *THE LAMB OF GOD*

Study II............................................ 14
   *THE ORDER OF MELCHIZEDEK*

Study III........................................... 27
   *THE FOUNTAIN FOR SIN*

Study IV........................................... 38
   *THE PLACE OF PEACE*

Study V............................................ 48
   *CHERUBIM OF GLORY*

Study VI........................................... 58
   *BE THOU MADE CLEAN*

Study VII.......................................... 72
   *FESTIVALS OF JOY*

Selected Bibliography.............................. 85

## LIST OF ILLUSTRATIONS

Photo of Model Tabernacle ........................... iii

The Twelve Tribes in the Hollow Square ............... 5

Mount Sinai with the Camp of Israel.................. 8

Plan of the Court in Elevation ....................... 28

Court with the Shadow of Christ ...................... 33

The Furniture in the Holy Place...................... 41

The Furniture in the Most Holy Place ................ 55

The Secular and the Sacred Months.................... 74

Chart of the Feasts .................................. 79

# Introduction

BY WAY OF introduction let me say that one of my main purposes in giving studies is to stimulate you to study the Bible for yourselves. You'll forget what I've said, but if you can get insight into methods, you can go home and read your Bible, gathering together the precious thoughts it contains. Then search the Spirit of Prophecy, a lesser light to point to the greater light. Your soul will be strengthened just as were the Bereans. They went home and studied to see whether the things the Apostle Paul said were so or not. In this spirit receive what is given here.

The Spirit of Prophecy tells us that the people of God who survive the time of trouble are only those who have made the Bible their counselor and the basis of their faith.* (*Great Controversy*, p. 593) Collect all the affirmative truths, all the statements that you understand clearly. By prayer and meditation on these inspired statements you will come to understand God's will for you. Resolve today that you are going to seek the Lord through a study of His Word, and God will bless your soul and bless your family and bless your witness as you have never yet experienced.

---

*Altogether too much time is spent in reading material that is unworthy, and looking at television that is many times more unworthy. If you spend two hours a day watching the television, you will have watched it for thirty days, in one year's time. You will be surprised what one hour a day will do for your study of the Bible.

# Study I

## THE LAMB OF GOD

THE GREATEST PRIVILEGE we can have is to study Christ. Every sermon should be an excuse for discussing Him. And yet, Jesus is one of the greatest mysteries the intelligences in the universe can contemplate. This very mystery was the basis of the success of Satan, because even the angels did not understand the true position of our Lord. The great controversies in the early church dealt with the nature of Christ. There is much discussion even now concerning His present ministry. The mysteries of godliness are to be subjects of study for the redeemed through all the ages which have no ending.

God has chosen many illustrations to help His people to understand the person, mission, and ministry of Jesus. The clearest and most important of them is the tabernacle. It is a wonderful privilege in freedom and peace, sitting in this commodious auditorium, through the help of the Spirit, day by day to seek an understanding of Jesus through the types and symbols of the sanctuary. Its services and sacrifices, its ceremonies and priesthood, designed by God Himself, help us to gain an intimate grasp of what our Saviour is doing in the heavenly sanctuary today.

David sang long ago, "In His temple every whit of it uttereth His glory." (Psalms 29:9 margin) Let us, by the help of the Spirit, examine the details of this tabernacle and hear the whispered message it brings of God's glory. This glory is the splendor of self-sacrificing love. Human ears may not be able to hear that utterance, but the Spirit will breathe it into hearts attuned.

When Moses first saw the glory in the burning bush, he rudely rushed in to investigate. But he was stopped by a voice crying, "Put off thy shoes from off thy feet, for the place whereon thou standest is holy ground." (Exodus 3:5) We should do this when we approach a study of the tabernacle. Many times the arrogant declare that nothing is symbolized by the details of the sanctuary. Rather should we say, "So far I have not seen what may be suggested. May the Lord give me insight." In this spirit of humble devotion, we are ready for God to open our eyes to help us discover wondrous things concerning our Lord depicted in the fabric and furnishing, the priesthood and ritual of the tabernacle. This is the passion play of the ages. It is a divinely sketched portrait of Jesus the crucified.

## The Plan of Salvation Revealed

Had there been no sin there would have been no sanctuary service. The fall made this necessary. The entire ritual had to be unfolded in fuller detail as man lost his powers of mind, originally so keen in Eden. Sometimes questions are asked regarding the value of a detailed study of the sanctuary. "Why, when we have the Christ of the New Testament, do we need to go back into the Old?"

I find no problem in the way of such a study. You have seen the beautiful illustrations in the books that are sold in the Christian Bookstores. Do you think that the artist painted these from memory? Why no! He used many models. Today these models, living and inanimate, need not sit for long hours before the artist. He simply takes colored transparencies of the sections of his picture by posing the model for a few minutes. When he is ready to paint, he works these segments together, studying each part in detail. It is for a similar reason that God has given us the details of the sanctuary. We should study each part minutely. Only then will we be able to see Christ in His fullness. We can comprehend only one point at a time. Jesus is the Sacrifice. He is also the priest. He is the Shekinah, and He is also the veil. He is "every whit!"

In order to discern the Lord Jesus Christ, the Lamb of God, the Mediator of mankind, the Saviour of the race, the Redeemer—King, we must synthesize all aspects of the tabernacle. While we may spend time on one part of His ministry, we should keep in mind that He is many-sided. It is only thus that we will come to understand "the One Who is altogether lovely, the chiefest among ten thousand," our Lord and Saviour Jesus Christ.

The Lord "drove" man out of the garden. (Genesis 3:24) The word means "divorced." The divine Bridegroom was forced to divorce His bride! When, with tear-drenched cheeks Adam and Eve, driven by sentinel angels, left their glorious home, God set up symbols of the plan of salvation that were later expanded into the model of the tabernacle erected by Moses.

At the gate of Paradise was seen the Shekinah. There were the Cherubim. There, too, was the lamb slain by the hand of Adam, its skin covering his nakedness. The altar was there to which Cain brought only a meal offering, while Abel also brought a lamb. He brought both, for there could be no burnt offering without a meal offering; For his refusal to obey, God rejected Cain's offering. For 1656 years at the cherubim-guarded gate of Paradise the righteous came to worship, bringing their sacrifices. (*Patriarchs and Prophets*, p. 62) It was by means of that gleaming sword, shining through hovering cherub wings, that the way to the tree of life was to be kept open. The word "kept" was first used by God in directing Adam and Eve to dress and "keep" their garden home. (Genesis 2:16) It means to preserve, observe and maintain. So the way to the tree of life was to be observed and preserved for those who would eventually find their way back to glory. When the Word became flesh, this glory was revealed fully, charged with "grace and truth." (John 1:14) With the sword, there are two edges to the Word—grace and truth. "Thy Word is truth," Jesus declared. The inspired Word reveals the theory of godly living. Grace is the power of Christ which enables us to practice the theory day by day.

At the Garden's gate God "placed" the cherubim. (Genesis 3:24) The word "placed" comes from the same root as "Shekinah." God's glory dwelt, as in light, between the wings of the cherubim. This glory illumined the road the sinner must travel back to God. It was here the true worshipers assembled. The Lord showed His acceptance of Abel's offering as fire flashed from the glory and consumed the sacrifice. The Shekinah could be a consuming fire. God asks the question, "Who among us shall dwell with everlasting burnings?" (Issaha 33:14) The answer is not the way Satan has made men believe, that the wicked burn forever! Only the righteous will dwell with God in glory. (Issaha 33:15–17) To live with light, we too, like the John the Baptist, must be "burning and shining," warming as well as illuminating. (John 5:35)

## The Lamb of God

In the initial story of the unfolding of the plan of salvation there is no mention of a lamb. We have to wait over two thousand years for a reference to this sacrificial animal. Let us follow a father and son as they journey from Hebron "to a hill far away." One morning a cloud gave them the sign which Abraham had seen in vision. Bidding his servants wait at the foot of Moriah, he and Isaac plod up the steep slope. On the way the boy asks his father, "Behold the fire and the wood: but where is the lamb for the burnt offering?" What was the old man to say to his eager boy? "My son," he replied, "God will provide Himself a lamb for the burnt offering." (Genesis 22:8)

They go the remaining few yards to the top. The explanations are made. Isaac helps the trembling fingers of his aged father to bind him to the altar he himself has assisted in erecting.

The last farewells are said. Abraham lifts the knife to kill his boy. Then comes from the throne a call from Christ Himself, "Abraham! Abraham!" Why do I say that Christ spoke? Because this is a personality trait. We find it recurring in the repeated names, "Martha, Martha," "Jerusalem, Jerusalem," and "Simon, Simon." An angel flies at Christ's behest to hold that plunging arm. The knife falls clattering to the ground. What tears of joy race down those two faces! Brushing them aside, Abraham looks and there is a ram with a crown of thorns. (Genesis 22:13) This he sacrifices in the place of his son. How thankful he must have been!

The question which rings through the ages is Isaac's, "Father, where is the *lamb?*" It is never answered in the Old Testament. We turn the pages between the Old and New and reach the same hill country. The descendants of the same father and son are there. The same query is on every pious tongue awaiting an answer. John the Baptist suddenly raises his arm and, pointing to Jesus of Nazareth, settles for all time the quest of humanity by his declaration, "Behold, the Lamb of God!" (John 1:29) Now the Lord has provided Himself, the Lamb for the offering.

## Israel Organized

While some details of the sanctuary system were given at the Garden of Eden, the fullness of revelation was not reached until Israel was encamped around Mount Sinai. Marshalled beneath its craggy brow were some three million people, just come from Egypt. They had pitched their tents in a large plain. The Lord called Moses into the mount and showed him a miniature model of the sanctuary in heaven, commanding him to supervise the erection of a similar structure, around which the entire life of Israel was to be organized.

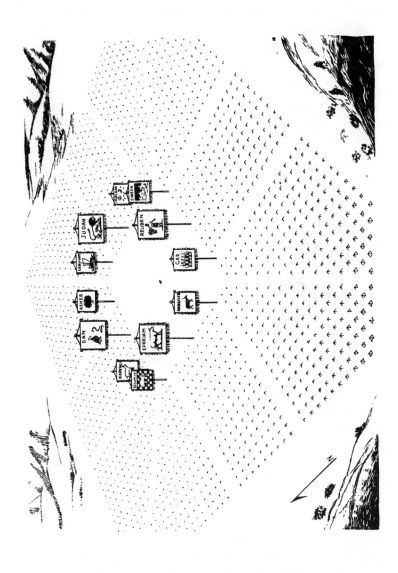

*The Standards of the Twelve Tribes and the Encampment*

At the time of the crisis connected with the golden calf the tribe of Levi had been selected for ministry, while the family of Aaron had been chosen for the priesthood. Twelve— tribes had been made up by honoring both sons of Joseph— Ephraim and Manasseh— with tribalship. The tribes were organized around the tabernacle in the form of a hollow square.

The organization of the tribes is described in the second chapter of Numbers. In the center of the square is the court and the tabernacle. The reason why artists have not illustrated it in this way is because the sanctuary appears so small. In most of the pictures you see, several scales are used—one for the encampment, another for the court, another for the tabernacle, and still another for the furniture. Because of this a very vital point is missed, that the distance from the edge of the encampment to the sanctuary was considerable.

To the east was the standard of Judah—a lion. (Genesis 49:9) To the south was the ensign of Reuben—a man. (Deuteronomy 33:6) To the west was the flag of Ephraim—a bull. (Deuteronomy 33:17) To the north was the sign of Dan—an eagle. Jacob had declared Dan to be a serpent. (Genesis 49:17) The Jews tell us that the men of Dan altered their emblem into an eagle, the killer of serpents! Thus around the camp were the lion, man, ox, and eagle. These four faces are seen in the cherubim. (Ezekiel 1 and 10; Revelation 4 and 5)

When the children of Israel marched they were to keep a distance of 2000 cubits between the ark and the first rank of the people. (Joshua 3:3, 4) It is understood by the Jews that the nearest the encamped Israelites were to come to the ark also was 2000 cubits. This would make the hollow square 4000 cubits to each side.

How long is the cubit? In the book, *Sanctified Life,* is a description of the golden image Nebuchadnezzar erected in the plains of Dura that was 90 feet tall. Daniel says it was sixty cubits. This would make one cubit equal one and a half feet. In the chapter of *Patriarchs and Prophets*, p. 347, which covers the sanctuary, we learn that this building was eighteen feet tall and eighteen feet wide. Exodus (26:16, etc.) informs us that it was ten cubits tall and wide. So one cubit equals 1.8 feet in contradistinction with the other cubit which equals 1.5 feet! But there is no problem. From Ezekiel 43:13 we learn that the cubit used in the sanctuary and temple was a special cubit. "These are the measures of the altar after the cubits. The cubit is a cubit and an hand breadth," the Lord says to Ezekiel.*

A cubit is the length from the elbow to the end of the middle finger. You can go to the East today and watch men selling cloth by the cubit. You will have lots of fun when a tall man comes to purchase material from a short store keeper. You will listen to Eastern politeness as they discuss who shall do the measuring! If the seller is a big man he will suggest the short purchaser measure. If, on the other hand, the purchaser is tall, he will want to measure and the storeman will demur. The sacred cubit is one hand's breath longer for good measure.

The 4000 cubit hollow square covered quite an area! The tabernacle would be two thirds of a mile from the nearest tents. This arrangement looked forward to the time when the twelve tribes of the redeemed of the Israel of God form a hollow square with Christ in the center.

Right in the middle of this cleared area the tabernacle was set up. It was surrounded by a court one hundred cubits long and fifty cubits wide, or 180 feet by 90 feet. The walls of this court were made of the purest white linen, and were nine feet tall.

This court yard was divided into two squares, as you see on page 28. Each was fifty cubits square. Into the eastern square the penitents might come. The common people were not permitted in the western square. In this only the priests might go. In the center of the eastern square stood the brazen altar, while in the middle of the westerly one was the ark. To the south of the medial line the laver was located. "Northward before the veil" was the place of sacrifice. (Leviticus 1:11) At right angles to the medial line were the three veils, one leading into the court, another into the holy and the third into the Most Holy Place.

The Holy Place also consisted of two squares, ten cubits to the side.(See Illistrations page 41) In the center of the more westerly

---

*When I see things like this in the Spirit of Prophecy, my faith is greatly strengthened. I have never found a statement of fact that deviated from the truth one hair's breadth in all Mrs. White's writings. I went through a crisis in my adolescence when I questioned the validity of the Spirit of Prophecy. I am always grateful for a godly Bible teacher who put his hand on my shoulder and said, "Leslie, before you make up your mind, read everything she has written." Now I have not done this yet! There are magazine articles and manuscripts that I still hope to read, but I have read her books, some many times. I have never found any discrepancies in any of her works.

*The Camp of Israel Arranged Around the Court*

square, the altar of incense was placed so that its four corners pointed toward the four points of the compass. To the north and south of the eastern square the table of shewbread and the seven-branched candle-stick stood. The Most Holy Place was a perfect cube. In the center of its floor the ark of the covenant rested alone. (See Illistrations on page 55)

Thus the plan of the tabernacle was based on a square. The court was made up of two squares. The Holy Place was also two squares while the Most Holy Place was one. Its shape was a cube. The new Jerusalem is in some ways the ultimate realization of the symbol of the Most Holy Place. Its length and breadth and height are all equal. (Revelation 21:16) At the heart of the city is the antitype of the ark, the throne of God. So there stretched from the Garden of Eden to Mount Zion a representation of the purposes of God for His people depicted through the symbolism of the tabernacle.

Picture if you will the millions of Israel gathered about Sinai. In the center of the encampment, arranged systematically tribe by tribe, is the tabernacle. It is surrounded by white linen curtains nine feet high enclosing the court. This curtain has an entrance only at its eastern end. Two thirds of a mile away in all directions the tents of the people are stretched.

## The Way of Cleansing

Let us imagine that somewhere in the camp a man sins. Conviction grips his heart. He must go to the sanctuary to gain cleansing! Picture him as he brings his sacrificial animal.*

He sets out from his tent across the open space, two thirds of a mile, in sight of all. Would it be presumptuous to imagine what his fellows were thinking? How fast gossip would start! Somebody might whisper to his neighbor, "I heard him quarreling with his wife last night, that's why he's going!" Somebody else might start for the tabernacle a

---

*I am asked, "How many offerings were presented by the Israelites?" How much would a bullock cost today? How many of you gave one offering to that amount last year. I don't think we are too different from ancient Israel! There would not have been too many of them who presented bullocks. How much would a sheep cost? A few of us may have given single offerings of this amount. You know, I think if we had lived in the time of Israel, we would have been out in the wilderness looking for turtle doves or young pigeons! The Lord understands our weaknesses and so provides sacrifices to meet all our needs.

couple of days after income tax returns were made and his neighbor would say, "His conscience is hurting him!" In spite of all this, the sinner must walk that distance by himself to find the way into the holiest of all by faith.

As he came nearer there stretched in front of him a white wall taller then he was, apparently without a break. What does fine linen symbolize? Yes, the righteousness of Christ. (Revelation 19:8) Somehow he must enter the shelter provided by this emblem of perfect purity. Imagine him standing before this curtain, wide and high. He can't see over it and so he passes along it, trying to find some chink. As he rounds its eastern side, he sees a curtain of different materials. It was made of wool, blue, purple and scarlet in color, together with fine-twined linen and gold. The old Talmudists say that the blue had a cast of green. Scarlet is the color of blood. Purple is a mingling of blue and scarlet.

In 1958 a Hebrew lady, Mrs. Amram spun these colors for me. She took the blue and the purple and the scarlet and the gold, as the Rabbis record that Bazaleel did. Six strands of blue and one of gold were separately spun. Then with one further strand of gold she twisted the three separate cords into a single strand. On a warp of fine linen she made a weft of this color combination. All the three veils were made of the same stuff, only their size and decoration were different. The veils leading into the holy as well as the Most Holy Place were ten cubits high and wide. But the veil from outside into the court was only five cubits high, while it was twenty cubits broad, it has the same area as the other two. The innermost veil was the most gorgeously embroidered with cherubim and palm trees.

## The Veiling of His Glory

While the sinner was still some distance from the eastern entrance veil, he would see above it the black skins covering the tabernacle. The Bible tells us that it was roofed with badger skins. The Hebrew word refers to a now extinct amphibious seal. (*Patriarchs and Prophets*, p. 347) In Song of Solomon (1:5) the king imagines he sees the tabernacle "black as the tents of Kedar." The sanctuary might be likened to a jewel-casket fifty five feet long, covered in black. It was not till the inside was seen, gleaming with gold, brilliant with the light from the golden candelabra and the splendor of the Shekinah that its true beauty was realized. Outwardly there was little beauty that we should desire it. Within its heart were wonders unfathomed. It is so with Him of Whom the tabernacle is a type.

But to return to the veil leading into the court. Of Christ's ministry Paul says that "He hath consecrated for us a new and living way though the veil, that is to say, His flesh." (Hebrews 10:20) The veil is therefore a symbol of the humanity of Jesus. Of His incarnation we read, "He pitched His tent among the tents of men and veiled His divinity in humanity." (*Desire of Ages*, p. 23) The human body of Jesus is the veil through which alone we can reach the glory of God, and by means of which the glory of God shines into our hearts.

Go out on a sunny day and look at the sun through your handkerchief. You will see through the interstices of the warp and weft the shinings of light. It is so with our Lord. If we look at the brilliant radiance of the sun with eyes unprotected, we would be blinded. If we saw the fullness of the glory of God, we should perish. So God has proposed, through the narrow space of the warp and the weft of the fabric of the humanity of Christ—of His life on earth—to reveal to us those rays of glory that our human limitations can see without being hurt.

So, as the penitent looks through the outer veil, he can see something of the glory which lies within. As the priest bids him enter the court, he will see a similar, though more luxuriously embroidered veil leading into the Holy Place. Christ is still the way here, as He has been the entrance. By faith the penitent can see the innermost veil, and the thought would be fixed in his heart that there was none other way under heaven, given among men, whereby we must be saved. (Acts 4:12) Jesus said in truth, "I am the way." (John 14:6)

In the court justification by faith is taught. Its furnishings and ritual illustrate this teaching. The only way to reach it is through the veil—Jesus Christ. In the Holy Place sanctification by faith is revealed. The only way to gain this is through the veil, Jesus Christ. In the Most Holy Place glorification is depicted and the only way to gain this is through the veil, Jesus Christ. Christ is the gateway to every stage of Christian growth. And when we get through the innermost veil into glory, then will be fulfilled the promise of our Lord to His church, "To him that overcometh, I will grant to sit with Me in My throne even as I am set down with My Father in His throne." (Revelation 3:21)

As the penitent with his offering reaches the outer veil, a priest is there waiting for him, who, like the Father, has seen him coming a long way off and has gone to meet him. Perhaps he puts his arm around him and says, "Son, find life and peace." The priest then lifts the veil and bids him enter through this multicolored symbol of the person of Christ. In the court he carefully explains to the sinner the meaning of what he sees. The priest himself is a type of Christ.

Before them is the brazen altar. From its top smokes the burning sacrifice. Before the altar is a pile of ashes. These are exposed for a while before removal, to emphasize that a full and complete sacrifice has been made. (*Testimonies*, Vol. 4, p. 120) They speak of penitents forgiven. As the priest leads the sinner south of the altar there will be seen the laver between altar and veil, slightly to the south. To the north stakes driven into the ground mutely tell of sacrifices bound to die. The entrance to the Holy Place is barred by another veil, but beyond it they can dimly discern the glories which can not be seen clearly. The priest who has seen this glory speaks to the sinner of what lies in the Holy Place.

The Shekinah, manifest to Moses in the burning bush, glowed in the tabernacle. The same acacia wood of the bush formed all the wooden parts of the sanctuary and its furnishings. Just as the bush was draped in splendor, so the tabernacle was irradiated with the glory of God. This glory had streamed on Sinai. As a pillar of fire it had led Israel through all their weary wanderings. Now it hovered over the sanctuary. Whenever it moved, the priests took down the tabernacle and with ark leading, followed the light. When the Shekinah stopped, they placed the ark below it, and erected around the entire tabernacle and encampment of Israel.

Jesus is that light and fire. Where he leads Israel must follow. Where He bids them stop they must pause. Around Him all the activities of His people should revolve. Fire accepted Elijah's sacrifice on Carmel. Fire descended at Pentecost in the form of cloven tongues to speak the Word. In the lives of the apostles, the Word, too, became flesh. Then that Word, incarnated in Christ, was incarnated in the church. Moses' face shone with glory. We beholding, may also become changed into the same glorious likeness of Christ from glory to glory.(2 Corinthinins 3:18) There was one glory in the court—justification; another in the Holy Place—sanctification; still another in the Most Holy Place— glorification. This glory is revealed to make us like Him—indescribable mystery! How may we, creatures of clay, men and women of sin—how may we be like Him? The radiance that shone from the acacia bush hid the leaves and branches from Moses' gaze. He saw only glory. The glorious grace of Jesus will hide our humanness, too, and reveal only His radiant likeness.

As the penitent stands in the court and contemplates all the possibilities which stretch before him, I imagine the priest explains to him some of the ways by which he might go from his tent of sin and meanness and iniquity, through stage after stage, through door after door that symbolizes Christ, until finally he stands in His presence unafraid, a privileged son of the King, a joint heir with Jesus sitting upon His throne for ever. (Revelation 3:21)

May God keep before us this glowing vision of possibility! May He strengthen us with power to put the theory of truth we know so well into practice day by day. May God illumine our minds with His Spirit to study each day the various aspects of Him Who is altogether lovely, the Chiefest among ten thousand, our Elder Brother!

# Study II

# THE ORDER OF MELCHIZEDEK

Today we study the priesthood. The word "priest" is a corruption of "prest," which itself is a contraction of "presbyter." This is the English form of the Greek word "presbuteros," meaning an older person, or an elder, the patriarch of the family to whom the others look with respect. Adam was the first priest. Abraham was a priest too, and so was Noah. The fathers of every family were priests until the time of the golden calf. Then Moses drew a line and said in effect, "All those who have been faithful to the Lord step to this side." The tribe of Levi responded. The Lord said, "Because Levi has been faithful, I will choose the priests from among them."

Centuries before, Levi had been cursed. In his dying prophecy Jacob had declared of Levi, "I will scatter thee in Israel." (Genesis 49:7) This curse proved to be a blessing! In taking the priests from the Levites and then scattering them among the tribes, God disseminated the ministry of reconciliation from the six cities of refuge throughout Israel. Next the Lord chose Aaron of the tribe of Levi to be high priest because he completely repented of his sins. As a result of this experience, Aaron was able to lead the rest of Israel into perfect penitence. His eldest son after him was to be the high priest while the rest of the sons of Aaron were the common priests. So the organized priesthood of Israel started.

## Basis of the Call to the Priesthood

But the tribes of Israel had the patriarchal system of priestly leadership behind them for a long time. In consequence a conspiracy against the Aaronic priesthood was stirred up by Korah, Dathan and Abiram. (Numbers 16) Dathan and Abiram were the first born of Reuben, who was the first born of all the tribes, including the tribe of Levi. Furthermore, Korah headed the tribe of Levi. If the priesthood was still to be based on birth, then one of these men should take Aaron's place. But the Lord settled this problem simply. He said in effect, "Each of you tribal leaders bring his staff of office inscribed with his name and, Aaron, you write your name on one, and we'll put all twelve rods before the ark." (Numbers 17:1–9) In one night that dead old stick of Aaron's budded, blossomed and produced almonds! And forever, by that miracle, was settled the dispute regarding the divine authorization of the Aaronic priesthood. He, in Paul's words, was no longer a priest by any carnal commandment, but his authorization was through the power of a resurrection life. (Hebrews 7:16) So with Jesus, His priesthood rests, not on any law of human genealogy, but on the power of a resurrection life too. That budding, blossoming and fructifying rod was placed in the seven-branched candlestick. (Exodus 25:33) Each branch of the candelabra was, as it were, an Aaron's rod in symbol. It was a type of new life, and upheld the lamps in the tabernacle. And so of Jesus, the antitype of the candlestick it could be said, "In Him was life, and that life was the light of men." (John 1:4) We will never uphold light until we have that life that first buds and blossoms and bears fruit to God. So the Aaronic priesthood rested on the new birth, on a new life, symbolized by the resurrection of a stick! And upon this regenerated life the mediation of the priest was based.

The priest must live an exemplary life. If he had any spot or blemish—a finger cut off or a foot injured or something wrong with him—he could not be the representative of the One Who is altogether lovely and utterly perfect. His diet was carefully regulated. He could not drink alcohol, nor was he to defile the body that in a special sense was a temple of the Holy Ghost. His wife was to be chosen with the utmost care. She was to be a member of the priestly family, and there was to be no stain or wrong living in her reputation. His place of abode was designated. There were six cities in which he was to choose to live. Those cities were placed strategically so that in times of emergency the children of Israel could come and obtain justice and instruction from the priests. "Cities of refuge." Wonderful name! The communities of priestly homes were "cities of refuge." In those six cities of refuge, the priests lived to administer justice. They were the judges. If a man by accident killed somebody and fled to the city of refuge for sanctuary, the priest was to protect him until his side of the story was heard. Then they must pass judgment in order that true justice might be administered. The death of the high priest cleared all penalties.

## The Order of Melchizedek

How many of His people did God design to be priests ultimately? Yes, every one of them! That is what He told Israel. "Ye are a chosen generation, a royal priesthood." Now Peter takes this text and applies it to all that come to Jesus Christ and are built up into a spiritual temple as living stones upon the foundation that no man can change. We all are to be "a chosen generation, a royal priesthood." (I Peter 2:9)

There is, however, no royal priesthood organized in the Bible. What tribe had the kings? Judah! What tribes had the priests? Levi! You can easily trace those two services—one of priestly ministry and one of regency—for centuries. In the second century before Christ, the Maccabees established the independence of the Jews in defiance of the Greeks and later of the Romans. Then for a period of some sixty years there were two kings who assumed the authority of the priests—only two, and they were criminals! The royal priesthood was a failure. But, yet, all Israel was to form such a priesthood. The Lord has given only one example, in the whole spectrum of the Old Testament, in whose life these twin rays of royalty and priesthood are blended successfully. Do you remember his name? Melchizedek! He was king and priest. Have you wondered why his name, Melchizedek was not translated? "Melchizhalom" has been translated, "king of peace" in Hebrews 7:12. But "Melchizedek" is not translated. It is transliterated, put into English characters. God wants to call particular attention to its significance. It means his kingdom is righteousness.

Melchizedek is the example of royal priesthood. When we, God's people, become kings and priests, it is not after the order of Aaron but it is after the character of Melchizedek.

In the fifth chapter of Hebrews, Paul tells us that no man took this office to himself but those who like Aaron were called by God. So the first point about this priesthood is that God calls. For the divine call to be effective, there must be a hearing and obeying ear on the part of Aaron and those who are called as he was. God invites us to enter His service. We sing the hymn, "Jesus calls us o'er the tumult of this life's wild restless sea." Jesus calls us all! When He had called Aaron, He told Moses, "Bring Aaron to the door of the tabernacle." How old was Moses when he was thus instructed? Eighty! His brother was two years older. We see those two brothers, walking step by step toward the east gate of the tabernacle. They lift the veil and enter the court, making their way to the laver. The Mishna tells us that the Levites had built a little enclosure to make the next part of the ceremony private. This ceremony is described in the 8th chapter of Leviticus. Having brought Aaron into this small pavilion by the laver, the Lord told Moses to take off his clothes and bathe him. Now, Aaron must have washed himself many times, but this washing he could not do for himself. It is a cleansing that only God can perform for mankind.

## Robes of Righteousness

Let us think about the laver. Of what was it made? Brass. Where did the brass come from? Yes, women who worshiped! What did they contribute? Looking glasses. Now, looking glasses are symbols of the law, according to James 1:24, 25. But can the law ever cleanse? Never! And so the Lord put in the laver the cleansing agency, the water of His Word. They went to the laver, and Moses washed Aaron. Then he dressed him with four special robes. They were each woven of fine linen. Aaron was to put on shorts from his waist to just above his knees. Over these shorts he was to wear a white robe that came just above his ankles, with sleeves to his wrists. Around his waist he bound a white belt or sash or girdle, as our Bible terms it. On his head he placed a turban wrapped round and round, with an end hanging down his back. This is called a miter. These were the four garments. Incidentally, they were also worn by the ordinary priest. Only once a year the high priest ministered in them. It was on the Day of Atonement that Aaron, clad in the garments of an ordinary priest, functioned on behalf of all the people in the Most Holy Place as a climax to the year's services.

Now these four garments, all of fine linen, represented Christ's righteousness. (Revelation 19:8) This foundation of the character of heaven was placed upon Aaron. He did not possess it inherently. He did not buy those robes. They were provided by God. He did nothing to obtain them. When he had been cleansed, he was dressed in them. They are emblems of righteousness that we do not earn that is given to us as a gift to cover the shame of our nakedness that results through our rebellion and sin.

Now, over those four white garments, the high priest had other garments that were for "glory and beauty." The first was a robe of blue wool, woven in one piece, reaching from his shoulders to below his knees. It was without sleeves. On the hem of this robe of blue were arranged golden bells and pomegranates. These pomegranates made of blue, purple, and scarlet wool in the shape of pompoms.

Over the blue robe Aaron was to wear a double apron made of the same material as the veils, —blue, purple, and scarlet wool, gold wire woven on a warp of fine linen. This was joined at the waist and on the shoulders, and was called the ephod. The ephod was embroidered with lilies. It was bound around his chest with a sash of the same material, blue, purple, scarlet and gold. The high priest was girded round his loins and round his heart. Bear this in mind when you read the promise of Christ's being doubly girded with righteousness and truth.

On his heart the high priest carried a breastplate made of the same materials as the ephod. It was two spans long and one span wide. Folded double it was a square span. Reinforced around its sides with gold, it was held to his shoulders with chains of gold and tied to the ephod by ribbons of blue. Upon his shoulders were two onyx stones. Chains connected the breastplate with these onyx stones. On the breastplate itself were twelve stones arranged in rows of three. These gems were engraved with the names of the twelve tribes of Israel. At the right and the left of these precious jewels were the Urim and the Thummim. Through these two gems God gave judgments and made decisions. Upon the four corners of the breastplate were four rings of gold through which ribbons were passed and tied at the back to hold the breastplate in position above the heart of the high priest.

Upon the shoulder onyx stones the names of the children of Israel were engraved, not according to the order of the tribes around the tabernacle as was the case in the twelve stones, but according to their ages. The six oldest were on the onyx stone to the right, and the six younger on the onyx stone to the left. Around the high priest's turban was a gold plate on which were inscribed the two words, "*Kodesh Ladonai*" or "Holiness to the Lord." Thus there were nine pieces to the high priest's garments —four white ones, then the blue robe, the ephod, the breastplate, the girdle and the plaque of gold on his turban.

All these garments are deeply symbolical. "Everything worn by the priest was to be whole and without blemish. These beautiful official robes represented the character of the great Antitype. Nothing but perfection in dress and attitude, word and spirit could be acceptable to God. Christ's glory and perfection were represented by the earthly services and priestly ceremonies. Finite man might rend his own heart by showing a contrite and humble spirit. This God could discern. But no rent must be made in the priestly robes, for this would mar the representation of heavenly things. Aaron's robes were symbolic. In all things we are representatives. The garments of the high priest were of costly materials and beautiful workmanship, befitting his exalted station." (*Desire of Ages*, p. 709)

## Symbolism of Color

Now, how shall we discover this symbolism? A starting point is given in Ezekiel 1:16—"The appearance of the wheels and their work like unto the color of a beryl..." This is a key text. Their work, the function they performed, was represented by color. On one occasion Ellen White had a dream where a green cord was handed down to her. When the dream was over she understood that the green cord had spoken hope to her heart. The message green has always given us hope. How many of you have seen a rainbow? Yes, we all have!

How many have seen a rainbow the color of an emerald? John did in Revelation 4. The Lord takes out all the other colors of the rainbow and concentrates on the one that should speak hope to our hearts when He describes the judgment scene in Revelation 4 and 5. How many have seen a rainbow that is a complete circle? They are rare. Most of them are semicircular. The rainbow around the throne of judgment completely encircles it with hope.

There is another color predominant in the sanctuary—blue. The children of Israel were told to put ribbons of blue on the hems of their garments and around their sleeves. What was that ribbon of blue to teach them? Faithfulness? Yes. Do you remember the statements that Ellen G. White makes or that the Bible makes? What were God's people to remember when they saw the ribbons of blue?—that they were God's people, that they were keeping His commandments. (Numbers 15:38–40; *Testimonies*, Vol. 1, p. 524) The Jews tell us that the two tables of stone given to Moses were of sapphire—blue.

This blue ribbon around the sleeves and around the hems of their garments was to remind Israel of the law of God. If I had a blue ribbon around my sleeve to remind me of the commandments of God, do you think I could cheat with this hand? There is nothing I can do with this hand that is wrong if I look at the ribbon of blue and remember the law of God. I have a fence about my feet so I can never take a step outside that ribbon of blue, outside the law of God. Bearing this in mind, I can not possibly go far wrong.

What does gold symbolize? "I counsel thee to buy of Me gold...,"(Rev. 3:18) the True Witness tells Laodicea. We find that gold represents faith and love—with love taking the precedence. Gold is yellow. Gold is used throughout the sanctuary weaving. Do you remember the story of how they made the gold wire? Bezaleel took gold pieces and beat them into flat plates. Gold can be beaten very, very thin. It can also be drawn through succeedingly smaller dyes. They knew how to draw gold in Egypt. But that was not the way Bezaleel had to make the wire, though it is the simplest method. He was told to beat the gold into plates and them cut then into strips with shears. These narrow strips he was to solder end to end, and so make a wire. Now, why did he do that? Gold represents faith. Does faith develop consistently without a break? No it does not! Mine does not! It grows a little while and then there is a break, and it grows a little while more and there is another break. That is what Bezaleel was taught. The development by faith is progressive and spasmodic, and linked by dark experiences.

## Words and Works

Over the white garments Aaron wore a robe wholly of blue representing God's law, and teaching that only on a basis of Christ's righteousness is obedience to the law possible. Around the hem of this blue robe were bells and pomegranates. Bells give sound and pomegranates are fruit. So are illustrated witnessing as well as obedience to the law of God; that in turn is based on a foundation of perfect purity—white under blue.

Over the blue robe was worn the ephod. In the ephod there are complicated ideas. The gold represents faith and love. This develops spasmodically, but the great craftsperson can make its growth continuous. He can join together our joyous experiences by little dark passages which might be represented by the solder. Then there is blue. This also represents the law of God. There is scarlet—the symbol of flesh, of humanity. And there is a blending of the scarlet and blue into the purple. I heard Campbell Morgan some years ago preach a sermon on a text in I Peter 1:6 about "manifold temptations." He coupled with it I Peter 4:10 which deals with "manifold grace." "Manifold" means many-colored. Look at the drapes at the back of me. They are crimson, but you will see streaks that are darker. These folds make many shades. There are manifold temptations and there are manifold graces. Morgan used an illustration from his boyhood. He had been given a box of colors and delighted himself in taking different pigments and mixing them together. Take blue and mix it with yellow and you get green. So, Morgan recommended that when you are feeling very blue mix it with the sunshine of the glory of God, yellow as gold, and you will find yourself in the green pastures of the Good Shepherd! Take blue and mingle it with scarlet, and purple will result. This is the color of priesthood, and speaks of Christ.

## Codified Love

The blue represents the ten commandments, the character of God —love. The ten commandments are codified love. The law shows what the truly loving will do in every circumstance. When God's character, expressed in Jesus, came down and combined with human flesh, our great high priest resulted. Paul says, "Forasmuch as children are partakers of flesh and blood, He also Himself likewise partook of the same." (Hebrews 2:14) Why? That He might become a faithful high priest. The ephod is made of blue, purple, scarlet, and gold—as are the veils of the temple—representing the humanity of Jesus Christ. The girdle of the ephod was made of the same material as the ephod. Our high priest's heart is girded with the feeling of humanity. And on the ephod the breastplate made of the same substance was bound.

On the breastplate the high priest carried the names of the twelve tribes of the children of Israel. And on his shoulders, upon the onyx stones, he also bore the names of the twelve tribes. What do you do with your shoulders? Carry burdens? When a father picks up his son and puts him on his shoulders, that little fellow can go through all dangers! So the high priest bears upon his shoulders the children of Israel. Now, what do you do with your heart? You feel, you sympa- thize, you understand. And the high priest bears the children of Israel on his heart. He gives them all the sympathy they need, he gives them all the power that they need. He carries them on his shoulders and upon his heart right into the presence of God. That is what he intends to do with each one of us.

To the right and to the left of the breastplate were two stones of greater brilliance than the twelve gems, called the Urim and the Thummim. The word Urim starts with aleph. This is the first letter of the Hebrew alphabet. In Greek the first letter is alpha. Thummim starts with tau. This is the last letter in the Hebrew alphabet and corresponds with the Greek last letter omega. The Urim and the Thummim represent the aleph and the tau. If you were depicting this idea in Greek, you would say alpha and omega or the beginning and the end.

We can express every thought within the compass of the 26 letters of our alphabet. So, the aleph to the tau; the alpha and omega; the A to the Z represents the vehicle for expressing each human thought. Jesus says, "I am the alpha and the omega." Within the compass of Jesus Christ, the Father expresses every thought that He wishes for mankind. Jesus is the Word. He is God's thought made audible, made visible, made tangible, made apprehendible, made incarnate.

Have you ever bought some gadget at the store and gone home and opened the package to read the directions? Have you ever become more confused as to how to work it than you were before reading the directions? But, then, you get somebody who has worked the device and he shows you how to do it. He puts those directions into practice. Now you can work the gadget, too! That is what Jesus did with God's directions for right living. He took all the rules that man needs in order to get out of this world alive and sit on God's throne, and He put them into practice. He is the Word incarnate, the Word made human. The theoretical directions are in the Bible. Jesus took all those directions and lived them as our example. He is the alpha and the omega, He is the A to the Z, He is the aleph to the tau. The Urim and the Thummim were vehicles through which God revealed His will to Israel of old.

## How Israel Cast Lots

You remember the instance when Achan stole things that did not belong to him? As a result the blessings of God were withheld, and when Israel attacked Ai, they suffered casualties. Joshua was desperately discouraged. He fell prostrate before the Lord and made his confession. The Lord said in effect, "Joshua, get up. It's time to do something! Get all the children of Israel before you—the twelve representative men—and by the process of elimination, discover who is the culprit." So, all the twelve tribes, by their representative men were lined up. The high priest stood there in all his magnificent attire. When the answer was, "no," a mist or cloud hovered over the stone Thummim. So, every question had to be put in such a way that it might have a yes or no answer. The twelve tribes stood there according to their seniority. Joshua, addressing God in the person of the high priest asked the question, "Is it Reuben?" The answer was, no! And so a little mist hovered over the stone Thummim. "Is it Simeon?" No! "Is it Judah?" And like an accusing finger a ray of light shot from the stone Urim. It designated the criminal. The tribe of Judah stood condemned. The other nine tribes, I imagine, sighed with relief, feeling smug and self-righteous. The culprit was being cornered. Now, the chief fathers of the tribe of Judah were lined up and slowly, inexorably justice was catching up with the criminal. At last Achan, the son of Carmi, the son of Zabdi, the son of Zerah of the tribe of Judah, was taken. (Joshua 7:18)

You will remember that when Saul and the children of Israel had problems after Jonathan ate honey, Saul said in effect, "We're going to settle this right now!" He put the royal family on one side and Israel on the other side to see where the crime lay. The high priest was there awaiting the question, "Is it Israel?" A mist covered the Thummim; therefore, it must be the royal family. Saul and Jonathan were placed before the priest and Jonathan was taken. Now, this process is called in the Bible, "casting lots."

God led His people by a pillar of light, Urim, and by a cloud, Thummim. Paul declared that in Jesus Christ all the promises of God are "yea and amen." When God commands we should say, " Amen." In Jesus all God's will for us should be "yea and amen." On the right of the breastplate there was a pillar of fire. To the left hand there was the cloud. God was leading His people. "Just as the high priest bears upon his heart the names of the twelve tribes of the children of Israel, so does our High Priest bear before His Father the names of every believing, repentant sinner." (*Evangelism*, pp.379, 380) Let me read another sentence: "In the breastplate of the High Priest there were many stones, but each stone had its special significance."(*Ibid.*) Have you ever spent time trying to discover what that significance is? I recommend that you do, especially you rock hounds. Get those twelve stones. They won't cost you much. I have a collection of them. The last time I showed them in public someone borrowed my ruby! If he happens to be in this audience, I would like it back! It is only a synthetic ruby anyway!

Each stone has a special significance. It is interesting that seven of these stones are made of silicon—sand. They all belong to the agate family. Three of the others are made of alumina. They have clay as their base. These gems are crystalline sand and clay. Crystalline quartz forms the amethyst and the topaz, the chrysoprasus and the agate, the plasma and the onyx, the sardonyx and the sardius. All these gems were in solution some time. That is the strange part of it—they were all in solution. Suddenly when saturation is reached, crystals form. So too, with the ruby, the sapphire and the topaz. The best rubies are found in Burma. Why did they crystalize there as rubies? Never after are these stones soluble in water.

## Character is Formed

What does water represent? "...peoples, and multitudes, and nations, and tongues." (Revelation 17:15) In the peoples and multitudes and nations and tongues, the clay that is going to form the jewels of God, is in solution. There is nothing to distinguish one particle from the next, one person from his neighbor. Suddenly the divine Alchemist causes crystallization. Characters are formed and thereafter they are never more affected by the solution, or environment, in which they happen to be. No one can ever predict where that crystallization will take place either in nature or life! You dig in mines and move tons and tons of dirt. Suddenly you come upon a gem! You move through thousands and thousands of people and suddenly Jesus will find one of His jewels. Chemically these gems are exactly the same as the clay and the sand, but the difference between a sapphire and the sardius and the clay and the sand is obvious. So it is with life. "Each stone has a special significance." And when Jesus said, "Let your light shine," He wanted the sapphire to shimmer with a blue color, and He wanted the topaz to glow with a golden gleam. He wished the plasma to emit a green sheen and He desired the amethyst to irradiate purple. The ruby does not quarrel with the sapphire or the topaz. Each gives out some special ray of the divine light and all together bring glory to the One who is the Light of the World. "Each stone has a special significance." Find out the tribes that were inscribed on the appropriate stones and you will discover that the natural history of each stone gives the perfect environment for the development of the character of that tribe engraved upon it. You will find, too, that whenever character is completely developed, the natural tribe and the spiritual apostle, which is his counterpart on the jeweled foundation of the city of God, reveal the character of Jesus. These ultimate apostolic characters stand forever on the foundations of the New Jerusalem as witnesses of God's transforming grace, guided by the light, denied by the cloud, borne on the breast of the high priest, reflecting the glory of the shekinah.

## Out Ministry

This priesthood reaches its fullness in the ministry of Melchizedek. The great question many people have grows out of the fact that he apparently had no father and mother. Ezra 2:61, 62 explains this to us. "The children of the priest.... sought to be reckoned by genealogy, but they were not found." That is, were without Levitical father and mother as far as the priestly records were concerned. The only man who could be a priest was one whose father and mother were named in the genealogy. The Ethiopic, the Syriac and the Arabic versions of Hebrews 7 say that "his father or mother was not found in the genealogy." How did Christ become a priest? Was His name found in the priestly genealogies of the Hebrews? No! Is your name found among the Aaronic genealogies? No! The priesthood of Melchizedek is the priesthood of the anonymous. Living in a pagan city, serving God as His representative, Melchizedek was called by God. Ellen G. White tells us that "God has never left Himself without witness on the earth. At one time Melchizedek represented the Lord Jesus in person to reveal the truth of heaven and to perpetuate the law of God. " Isn't that what we're to do—reveal the truth of God and to perpetuate His law? "It was Christ that spoke to Melchizedek, the priest of the Most High. Melchizedek was not Christ. He was the voice of God in the world, the representative of the Father." (Letter 190, 1905; Review Herald, Feb. 18, 1890) She adds, "As soon as David was established in the throne of Israel, he began to plan for a more appropriate position for the capital of his realm. Twenty miles from Hebron a place was selected as the future metropolis of the kingdom. Before Joshua had led the armies of Israel over Jordan to the promised possession, it had been called Salem. Near this place Abraham had proved his loyalty to God. He had prepared an altar, and had laid upon it his only son Isaac, in obedience to the command of the Lord. Here had been the home of Melchizedek, the priest of the most high God, nearly nine hundred years before the coronation of David. It held a central and elevated position in the country, and it was barricaded by an environment of hills. On the north rose Lebanon, with its snow-crowned summits.... In order to secure this much-desired location, the Hebrews must dispossess a remnant of the old Canaanites. King David called for men to besiege and take the city, and the capital was moved to Jebus. This heathen name was changed to the city of David, and it was afterward called Jerusalem, and Mount Zion." (*Signs of the Times*, June 22, 1888, pp. 136, 703)

We as Christians are part of the priesthood of Melchizedek. This is the ministry of the anonymous believer, responding to the call of God, bearing the burden of the jewels of God on our hearts and on our shoulders, as God's great high priest did. We must be washed with the washing of the water by the Word, clothed with the fine linen of the righteousness of Christ, surmounted by the blue of obedience, bringing forth fruit in witness, with our heads crowned by right thinking, marked with the holiness of God. That is a picture, first of the Lord Jesus Christ, and then a picture of what we should be. May God help us to fulfill that vision.

# Study III

## THE FOUNTAIN FOR SIN

THIS MORNING WE shall study what happens in the court of the tabernacle. You remember we left the penitent, bringing his offering and being met at the door of the sanctuary by the priest. We have spent some time thinking about the priest, about his regalia and the meaning of his ministry. Without the priest the ritual of the sanctuary would be pointless because then there would be no one to minister the blood. The mediation of the priest is vital.

### The Priest of God

The priest was a man who understood by experience the needs of his people. Christ could not become a priest until He had become a man. That is Paul's argument in Hebrews. His conclusion is: "Forasmuch then as the children are partakers of flesh and blood, He also likewise took part of the same…. that He might be a merciful and faithful High Priest." (Hebrews 2:14, 17) The incarnation of Christ is the essential prerequisite. No man from Mars, not even the Holy Spirit, could be a priest of the Most High God. The priest, Melchizedek, must be a man.

Pentecost was the sign that Christ's inauguration as our High Priest has been completed in the heavenly courts. (*Acts of the Apostles*, p. 39) Now, I know that Jesus Christ is "the Lamb slain from the foundation of the world," (Revelation 13:8) but He died 1900 years ago. I know that Jesus Christ is "a priest for ever after the order of Melchizedek," (Hebrews 5:6) but He was inaugurated 1900 years ago. While in the mind of God, Christ's entire ministry is eternally established, as far as man is concerned, it functions in time.

So the priest, touched with the feeling of the penitent's infirmity, (cf. Hebrews 4:15) met the sinner there at the eastern entrance to the court of the tabernacle and led him through the symbolism of the articles of furniture in the court and in the Holy Place, helping him to carry out his part in the services.

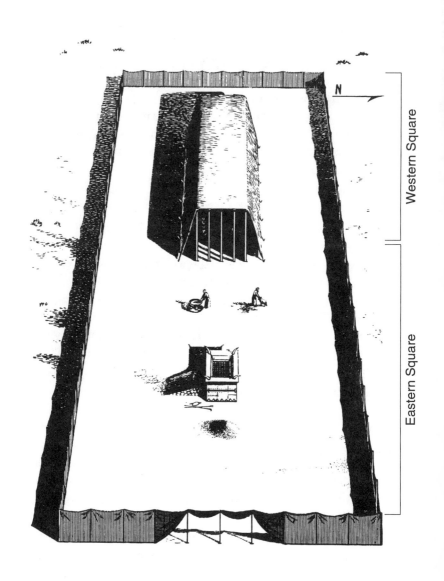

**The Court of the Tabernacle and Its Furnishings**

## The Lamb of God

Watch the penitent bringing his offering, be it bullock, lamb, turtle dove, pigeon, or if he could not afford that, a handful of flour. For our illustration, suppose that he brought a lamb—an innocent small creature. He leads it south of the altar and the laver, northward of the medial line, to a place somewhere before the veil. Look in the model and you will see the arrangement clearly. Standing at the place of death he lays his hands on the head of the victim. The Hebrew means that he leaned his full weight upon it. Picture a 200-pound man crushing a tiny lamb down to the earth! There was no floor to the sanctuary. God came down to earth to illustrate His plan of salvation. Can you see that little creature crushed, perhaps bleeding, with the weight of the sinner bearing him down? Let your minds encompass the scene of Jesus Christ, crushed and bleeding as the weight of the sins of the whole world are laid upon him. And then, in silence, the penitent confesses his sins to God.

When he has completed his confession, the priest hands him the knife. The animal is bound, the neck is stretched so that the face of the lamb is turned toward the Most Holy Place. In one stroke the penitent cuts the animal's throat with his own hand. So *I* put the Son of God to death! Not the soldiers 1900 years ago; not Caiaphas nor Pilate, not the centurion, *I* cause Calvary. God be merciful to me! The Bible says *we* crucify the Son of God! (Hebrews 6:6)

## The Priest Applies the Blood

The priest catches up the blood in a golden bowl as it flows from the dying victim. As far as the sinner is concerned, that is the end of his part. All he can do is to slay the Lamb—to "crucify the Son of God afresh." (Hebrews 6:6) There is nothing else he can bring. His sin has wages—death! Following the sacrifice the priest must take over, and do for the repentant sinner what he cannot do for himself.

There were different kinds of offerings. (See Leviticus 4) In that presented by individuals the priest partook of the victim, identifying himself with it. (Leviticus 6:25, 26) So Christ, Himself the priest, Himself the offering, shared the lot of the dying sinner. One of the questions that is often asked is: "How would the priest be able to eat all those sacrifices?" According to Rabbinic practice all he had to eat was a piece as big as an olive. There are some who think that this is a sanction for us to eat flesh. The symbolism is that the priest and the victim must be identified. The sacrifice mast become part of him, bone of his bone and flesh of his flesh. This ritual illustrated 2000 years before it came to pass, that Jesus was to take upon Himself humanity, that our flesh was to become part of His flesh.

In different sin offerings the blood might be ministered in two ways. It might be taken within the Holy Place and sprinkled before the veil. Some blood drops would get on that veil. Paul tells us that the bodies of those victims whose blood was brought within the tabernacle were burned outside in a clean place. (Hebrews 13: 10, 11; Leviticus 6:30) This indicated that Jesus Christ died, not only for the Jews but for the whole world. (*Testimonies*, Vol. 4, pp. 120–123) The application of the sacrifice of Christ is not only to Israel but also to sinners every-where. So when the blood was brought inside, the body was burned outside.

But if the priest ate a token portion of the offering, the remainder of the body was burned on the brazen altar in the court. (Leviticus 4:30, 31) Now I am going to synthesize all the kinds of offerings, because we don't have opportunity to study the differences between the burnt, the sin, the trespass, the peace and the meal. Very, very suggestive lessons are taught by them all. The priest first had to take the skin off, and then he had to dissect the animal. Paul uses that term when he tells us that we should rightly divide the "Word of truth." (2 Timothy 2:15) That is the expression taken right out of the sanctuary language. The victims had rightly to be divided—the head separated from the body, the legs and the tail cut off, the intestines removed, and the body cut in two.

Then each part had to be washed. When Paul says, "Cleanse it with the washing of the water by the Word," (Ephesians 2:6) the word he uses for "regeneration" in Titus 3:5 is "laver." We are washed by the "laver," through the Word. That is why the Word must be applied constantly. It would be wonderful if my shirt could be washed once forever wouldn't it? My shirt has to be washed every single day. The water has to go through it repeatedly. That is what the Word has to do with my heart. It cleanses it. When we allow the ideas of the Divine Word to pervade our minds, though we may not remember 100th part of what we have heard or read, that very process will wash our minds and cleanse them. And so, the body of the offering had to be washed in its sections before it could be presented upon the altar and accepted by God.

## The Victim on the Altar

Next the priest took up the various parts of the body, went to the south side of the altar and ascended the ramp. There in front of him were the logs that were to consume the offering. Now, what was the wood used? The Mishna tells us (the Mishna is the Jewish commentary on the Old Testament ritual) that the preferred wood was from the fig tree. Why the fig tree? What did Adam and Eve do with the fig tree? They pulled some leaves off and made the first hula skirt! It wasn't very good. It wasn't very lasting. The fig tree is mentioned several times later in the Bible.* Look up the Bible references to the fig tree, and God will speak to your heart.

With the fig tree in the Garden of Eden providing leaves, we learn the lesson that the leaves of a fig are to be associated in our minds with man's own efforts to make up for his sinful nature by his own works. Christ told a parable about a fig tree. He said it was planted in a vineyard and that the owner of that vineyard came for three years looking for fruit. He did not find any and was ready to cut it down. But the gardener intervened, "Let it alone this year also till..." (Luke 13:6–8) What was the total time for probation of that fig tree? Four years! The ax had been laid to the root of the tree when John the Baptist began to preach. (Matthew 3:10) How much before Jesus Christ began His ministry did John begin? Six months. How long was Christ's ministry? Three and a half years. If you add six months to the three and a half years, you get four. At the end of four years, what did Jesus do to the fig tree that did not produce fruit? (Matthew 21:19, 20) He rejected it. It died! The ax had threatened it four years before. When

---

*Buy a good concordance. Don't buy a Bible with a concordance in it. They are the most frustrating inventions that were ever attached to a Bible. I have never found in a concordance attached to a Bible any verse I wanted to find—it was always missing! It adds too much weight to the Bible, and you will find that a Bible with a concordance breaks down. Now, the Bible my Mother and Father gave to me in 1930, has been bound twice. In the first 30 years of service, it is an excellent Book. I never mark the Bible, because what I want to mark today I find does not impress me next year. So, get a good Bible with good marginal references, and then buy a good concordance. With these tools, collect the verses on the subject you wish to study, lay them down in front of you and meditate on them prayerfully.

it failed to bring forth anything but leaves, the sustaining power of God's grace was removed. (*Desire of Ages*, pg. 583) So it died because it represented pretensions only, words without corresponding deeds. The fig in the Bible is a symbol of self-righteousness, of hypocrisy, pretense; and when you read the gospel stories, you will discover that nothing burned up the Lamb of God so much as hypocrisy! So, on the brazen altar the fig logs were placed to indicate that it is man's pride which brings the Lamb to His destruction.

We watch the priest as he heaves the parts of the offerings on the altar. He puts them there any way they happen to fall. When he has placed on the altar all the portions that were to be consumed, he takes the flesh hooks and arranges the offering to look like the animal. He places the head at one end. Then he puts the two flanks, the two front legs, the two back legs and the tail all appropriately. This is to teach us that when we first place ourselves on the altar, (Romans 12:1, 2) we may seem to be completely confused. Life may be mixed up. But if we will have patience, we shall discover that the great High Priest will arrange us in perfect order! So, "let us bring our bodies as living sacrifices," (Romans 12:1) which is our reasonable service. Let us do this daily. We will find out that the confusion, uncertainty, and everything connected with our dedicated bodies will be completely resolved.

## The Offering Accepted by Fire

When the victim was rightly divided and properly arranged, the fires of divine acceptance descended on the altar. The first time Moses set that altar up, the fire of God descended, lighted the logs and began to consume the offering. "Our God is a consuming fire." (Hebrews 12:29) Fire is a symbol of the Divine Presence that purges and accepts. It burns away the dross, yet it illuminates and makes incandescent the true gold. Thereafter, in all Israel's wanderings through the wilderness, a priest was assigned to keeping this fire alight. Ellen G. White tells us that he did so by adding incense to the coals. Incense is a symbol of the merits and intercession of Christ, which, added to the prayers of the saints, make them acceptable before the Lord. So the fires were to be kept alive every day by His intercession. The illuminating spark of Calvary will ever glow upon the altars of our hearts through prayer.

Each time the priest went to the altar he washed his hands and his feet at the laver. In the morning he had a bath. Thereafter, every time he went into the Holy Place or ministered about the altar, he washed only his hands and feet. So. "He that is washed needeth not save to wash feet, but is clean every whit." (John 13:10)

We may see in the court three items of particular significance. In the center is the brazen altar with the wood and the fire and the victim. To the south is the brazen laver, made of the mirrors of the women who came to worship. To the north is the place of sacrifice. At these three points of interest the method of God's dealings with sinners is illustrated. By fire, water, and blood our justification is achieved. Jesus told His disciples at the Feast of Tabernacles, "If any man thirst, let him come unto Me and drink...the water I shall give him shall be in him a well of water springing up into everlasting life...this spake He of the Spirit." (John 7:37–39;4:14) Water is a symbol of the Spirit. Fire is an emblem of our God who "is a consuming fire." (Deuteronomy 4:24; Hebrews 12:29) Blood is a token of the human life which the incarnate Son of God poured out on Calvary. These three symbols

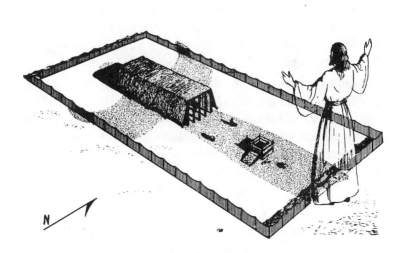

*Shadows of the Christ*

of the heavenly Trio, who work in unison to bring about the justification of the sinner, are seen in the court.

As we think of these symbols, there shine into our hearts rays of light, clarifying the purposes of God. We see the penitent stand in the midst of that threefold provision. He has nothing to present. His hand is dripping with the blood of the victim. The knife is there. He is the murderer of God! But there is built for him, by fire and water and blood, a platform on which he may stand just before God. When we come and accept this provision, when we take what is meant by the fire and the washing and the blood, then our journey to heaven is begun and our way into the holiest of all made open for us.

What does the sinner do as he stands there? He watches the priest eat part of the sacrifice, identifying himself with the victim as Jesus was Himself the Priest, Himself the Offering. He watches the sacrifice presented before God. He sees God take it to Himself and identify Himself with it in that flame. The offering and God are blended. Thus man is justified. Justification is the work of a moment. It is the work of God. Man can do nothing about it. It is done for him. All man can do is to come and acknowledge that he has slain the Lamb of God because he has sinned. By the services in the court, justification by faith is taught. So the penitent learns the initial lesson of Christianity.

At this point the priest takes over. He carries a bowl filled with blood. What does this symbolize? God says, "The life of the flesh is in the blood." (Leviticus 17:11) So the priest has in his hand a symbol of *life*. He takes this blood into the Holy Place. Let us watch him inside the Holy Place as he sprinkles it before the veil.

As the priest stands in the Holy Place, he sees to his left the seven-branched candlestick, to his right the table of shewbread, and in front of him the golden altar of incense. We shall have time for only a brief consideration of the seven-branched candlestick. It is described in the 25th chapter of Exodus.

## The Candlestick

The seven-branched candlestick was made by Bezaleel out of one piece of gold weighing a talent. He was told specifically that he was to make it with beaten work. It might have been poured into a mold and this would have been simpler. In order to make it with beaten work, the gold must be heated and allowed to cool, then it could be beaten with a hammer. It must be annealed again in the fire and beaten again. This process is kept on tens of thousands of times. If the metalsmith stops annealing the gold it becomes crystalline and cracks into pieces. So Peter declares, "Beloved, think it not strange concerning the fiery trial which is to try you, as though some strange thing happened unto you." (I Peter 4:12) The fiery trial makes us amenable to the hammer of the Word. It shapes us. (Jeremiah 23:29) So Bezaleel took this fine gold that represents faith and love, and he annealed it and beat it and made it into the form of a lampstand.

The candlestick had a central shaft, with three branches going out at each side. The branches included the likeness of a bud, a blossom and an almond. This motif is seen in Aaron's rod that was resurrected. (Numbers 17:8) It is the symbol of the new, regenerate life that brings forth buds, blossoms and fruit—almonds. Christ said of this process, "First the blade, then the ear, after that the full corn in the ear." (Mark 4:28) It suggests every stage of Christian development. At each stage we must be perfect in our sphere as God is in His.

Now, how tall is this seven-branched candlestick to be made? The Bible does not tell us. We are told how tall the altar of incense is and how tall the table of shewbread is, but we are not told how tall the candlestick is. That was left up to Bezaleel. How high do you want to lift the light? That's up to you, too! God's ideal is higher than the highest human thought can reach, but it is up to you to reach it. Bezaleel could make the candlestick just as tall as he wanted to. We, too, can lift the light up just as high as we will permit God to strengthen us.

At the end of each of these branches was a lamp shaped like an almond, a hollow dish. It had a peg beneath that fitted into a hole in the top of each branch. Each lamp could be taken off and oil and a new flame affixed. I was interested for years to discover where the wicks came from. The Mishna says that the used robes of the priest were used for this purpose. They were torn into ribbons and plaited into wicks. Now, tell me, what does the white robe of the priest suggest to your mind? The fine linen is the righteousness of Christ! It is this that glows in shining glory in the darkness of this life!

Oil is a symbol of the Holy Spirit. So it is the righteousness of Christ, saturated with the oil of the Holy Spirit, that is the agent of illumination. Where does the fire come from? Mrs. White tells us that the spark to ignite the light was brought from the brazen altar. The brazen altar is a symbol of Calvary. Here is the statement: "Everyone that kindles his taper from the divine altar holds his lamp firmly. He does not use common fire but the holy fire, kept burning by the power of God day and night." (*My Life Today*, p. 217) Each soul is to light his own taper. What is this taper? Solomon says, "The spirit of man is the candle of the Lord." (Proverbs 20:27) You must light your taper at that altar too. And with the righteousness of Jesus Christ clothing you, filled by the oil of the Spirit, your life will be made incandescent by the glory of Calvary. You may lift that glory up on the branches, symbols of the resurrection life, just as high as you want!

## The Talent

What is the only measure connected with this seven-branched candlestick? One talent. Christ told a story about talents. What did the fellow do that had one talent? Make a candlestick out of it? No! He buried it in the ground, after he had wrapped it in a napkin! It wasn't that he hid it. He dedicated it to pursuits of this earth. But Bezaleel made the most beautiful symbol of the Christian that you will find out of this talent of gold. We have the same choice.

How often was this candlestick lighted? Every morning and evening. Who was to light it? The priest who is a representative of Jesus. The candle of our lives, "the spirit of man," must be lighted morning and evening by Jesus Christ. What is our spirit? Shall I illustrate? You are just coming to church some Sabbath. You have spent a long time washing your white skirt that has 378 pleats in it! You have ironed it perfectly. It has rained earlier that morning. As you are about to enter your car an automobile goes through a puddle and your white skirt is no longer white! It is at junctures like this that you demonstrate what spirit is in you! Then you come to church. You are parking your brand new automobile and somebody opens his 25-year old jalopy and you no longer have a perfect paint job! What spirit do you show? When the poor fellow in front of you has a reaction time to the red light $\frac{1}{500}$ of a second less than yours, do you indulge in electronic swearing by means of your horn? "The spirit of man is the candle of the Lord." It must be lighted morning and evening by the High Priest or it will spark with fire of mere human kindling!

## Putting Out the Light

Jesus talked a great deal about allowing our light to go out. He uses three illustrations. He says that we may hide our light under a bushel. (Matthew 5:15) With bushels we measure our harvests. A bushel is a symbol of human standards of material success. We can allow materialism to put our light out. What else did He say might put out the light? A bed!(Mark 4:21) A bed is a symbol of two things—laziness and lust. We can allow both to put the light out. Where else did He say we might put out the light? In a secret place! (Luke 11:33) A secret sin can snuff out the light. But where should we place the light? On the candlestick. What is the candlestick? The church. (Revelations 1:21) There are some people who think they can let their lights shine apart from the church, but they can't. We break Christ's specific commandment when we try this. When the Lord illumines the candle of our souls, He wants us to add our spark to the light already shining from His church.

When the priest lifted up the veil into the Holy Place and the penitent saw the lamp, he saw there a symbol of what God intended him to be through Jesus Christ. We must catch this vision. Therefore, He says to you and to me, "Let your light so shine." (Matthew 5:16) When the priest went inside to take the blood to sprinkle it, when he lifted the veil, it was only then that the interested penitent might look inside. Calvary gives us insights nothing else can.

Has God lighted the taper of your soul? Have you brought your spirit and allowed the spark of Calvary to illuminate you? Have you brought the righteousness of Christ and allowed the Holy Spirit to saturate it with the oil of gladness in your heart? Are you allowing the fires to relight the lamp of your soul each morning and evening? Paul urges us, "...Be not conformed to this world: but be ye transformed by the renewing of your mind." (Romans 12:2) That word "renewing," in the Greek, is used in the sanctuary service for relighting the seven-branched candlestick. Your mind must be relighted morning and evening by the afterglow of Golgotha.

May God make us willing to submit to the daily ministry of our High Priest.

# Study IV

## THE PLACE OF PEACE

CHRIST IS THE LIGHT of the world. So is the church. So should we be. The initial igniting spark of our light is from the altar of burnt offering. This is an emblem of the sacrifice of Christ on Calvary. There are no windows in the tabernacle. So the only light in the Holy Place was the seven-branched candlestick. In this apartment we are taught the truth of sanctification by faith. The seven-branched candlestick stood on the south side of the Holy Place. It represented Jesus who is the only source of our light. We should walk in the light of His illumination. Jesus is our guide in living the life of true sanctification.

To the north of the Holy Place stood the table of shewbread. Its legs were curved. Josephus tells us that the table had legs similar to those the Dorians had on their beds. A little research will disclose that Doric bed legs were an imitation of the legs of a sheep. This the French call "cabriole."

### The Unleavened Bread

On the table twelve loaves of bread were always placed. The table was provided with rods to carry it. These rods were across the short ends of the table. The front of a table is the longer edge. On the march the priests put the rods on their shoulders and carried the table with the loaves of bread upon it. *Patriarchs and Prophets* tells us that incense was sprinkled between each of these loaves, six to a pile, and that on the top of each was a golden dish containing "frankincense." (Leviticus 24:7) What does the word "frank" mean? Open, honest, outgoing, not secretive and retiring. Frankincense was the gum the incense plant exuded spontaneously when the sap was rising. It was perfectly clear. Later they made incisions in the bark of the tree in the same way incisions are made in pine trees to get turpentine. The sap that came out was thicker and darker. The piece I have is speckled and completely opaque. Frankincense represents the freely given merits and intercession of Jesus which makes our prayers acceptable. These merits, like the cross, are stamped on each loaf of bread. So incense was sprinkled upon the shewbread. This, like the meal offering, and the bread of the paschal offering, was made of whole wheat flour mingled with oil, with a touch of salt. The recipe is given in the second chapter of Leviticus.*

The shewbread was prepared each Sabbath. The Mishna says that golden rods were placed between each loaf or cake so the air could get through and prevent moulding. There were twelve loaves because there were twelve tribes. God prepared this bread in sufficient quantity for all His people just as He later multiplied the loaves and gave them to the twelve to distribute to the people. The incense represents the merits and intercession of Christ. These are portrayed so magnificently on Calvary's cross. When the shewbread was taken away on Sabbath morning to be eaten by the outgoing priests, the incoming priests, having prepared their contribution of the shewbread, placed the loaves on the table. When the shewbread was removed, priests took the incense in the bowls on each pile of loaves and offered it on the golden altar as thanksgiving before the Lord for His goodness. So the cross of Calvary is stamped on every loaf of bread. It is because Jesus Christ's merits and intercession are given to us that we are not destroyed and that the divine blessings are multiplied to us every day.

Now, think a moment on how this bread was prepared. The wheat was put into the soil. It died. It rose again, brought forth some sixty fold, some eighty fold, some a hundred fold. It was then reaped, threshed, and winnowed. The grains were put between the upper and nether millstones and they were ground. The flour was mingled with

---

* I'd like to call attention to a very interesting point. There were three ways of preparing this bread. It could be baked in an oven. It could be fried in a frying pan, or it could be cooked on a griddle. I would like some enterprising deaconess for some communion service to fry the bread! I've had baked communion bread ever since I started to partake of the communion. It would make for variety; the idea is Biblical. Another way is to cook it on a griddle. In the Middle East, as I did in India as a boy, we ate bread like this often, cooked on a griddle. My wife prepares bread like this now. Those of you who have been to India will remember the "chapati," and you will remember the "parata," too. One is prepared on a griddle and the other is fried. The Lord allowed the different ways to make for variety. I think that church deaconesses who go and buy the white flour preparations that are prepared commercially and are eaten now in the Passover are almost committing crimes against humanity! I seriously think that in our churches we ought to have changes, as God allowed the bread to be changed. Read the texts in Leviticus 2:4–7 and see what the Lord has said. Why not try it sometime?

oil. Salt was added. This represents the character of Jesus Christ. Fire was applied. Only then was it presented to the Lord. Before it could be eaten it must be broken. Finally the priests partook of it. It became bone of their bones and flesh of their flesh. The bread and priests were identified completely. Each Sabbath day this bread was to be new. Thus is the Bread of Life. The Word that we preachers proclaim should be the Bread of Life.

Let us imagine that we have opened the veil and that we are looking into the Holy Place. To the left, as you will see in the model on page 41, is the seven-branched candlestick. To the right is the table of shewbread. One gives you light; the bread gives you strength to walk in the light. The one shows you the path you should travel, the other empowers you to travel. Every sermon should be just like that. It should have within itself illumination, vision, insight, inspiration. It should also have in it the basic material on which faith is formed. How will men get faith except they hear the Word of God? So every sermon should tell what to do, and should also have within itself the source of the power to carry it out.

In the court, justification was taught. Man is forgiven his sins, his record is clean. He has left behind him all the sinfulness of his past life. He is now starting anew. He is a babe. His eyes have just been opened, and, as by faith, he enters the Holy Place, the shining candlestick helps him to see the road he must travel. He can stretch out his right hand, and get bread to strengthen him in that travel.

By the side of the table of shewbread were flagons of wine. There must be no meal offering without its corresponding drink offering. The two go together—always bread and wine. In the Passover there was bread and wine, in the communion service there is bread and wine. The wine is the product of the fruit of Jesus Christ. He is the true vine. There are two wines in the Bible. There is the "true wine," and there is the "wine of the earth." There are two wines in the Bible—the new wine, and the wine of the wrath of Babylon's fornication, the false doctrine that results from the force imposed by the unlawful union of church and state—the compromise that Babylon makes. There are two kinds of doctrine. Jesus lifted up the cup containing the wine, and He said, this wine is the new covenant in My blood which is shed for you for the remission of sins. (Matthew 26:28)

*The Holy Place*

## The Covenants

I've been asked whether I will talk about the two covenants. I hadn't planned to, but I would like to make just a statement in passing. The old covenant is the old covenant, and the new covenant is the new covenant. The old covenant, being the old covenant, started before the new covenant which is the new covenant! The old covenant has as its basis the truth, "obey and live; disobey and die." The angel Gabriel lives under that old covenant. He obeys and he lives. Should he disobey, he would die. Lucifer disobeyed, and Lucifer will die. Adam and Eve lived under the old covenant — "obey and live; disobey and die." The inhabitants an other planets are still living under the old covenant—they obey and live. If they disobeyed, they would die. Adam and Eve failed. Death passed on all flesh. Now there came into operation the new covenant. Jesus said in effect, "I will help you obey that you may live and not die." That is the new covenant. There is nothing complicated about it. We sometimes make it complicated. The new covenant has the same basis as the old, obey and live, only Jesus helps us to obey when we are powerless.

You and I may enter into the old covenant at any time. I was given the privilege a little while back to work with the pastor of the first church in Baltimore in an evangelistic series. One time he said, "Let's go over and see Mr. _____." So we drove to his house and discussed cigarette smoking. Our friend said, "Yes, I know it is time I gave up smoking. I can give it up anytime I want to." Whenever I hear somebody say that a cold shiver runs down my spine, because I know better. He cannot give up smoking in his own strength. This fellow could not! When Israel said, "All that the Lord hath spoken we will do," (Exodus 19:8) they were operating under the old covenant. They failed, in their own inability, to do what God decreed. They realized their incapacity to do God's will for the first time. They needed to learn this lesson: that fallen man can no longer live successfully under the old covenant. He cannot obey! So Jesus has ready for us the new covenant in which He promises us His all-sufficient grace to enable us to obey. Praise the Lord! The cup in communion is a symbol of the power of that new covenant through the blood of Jesus Christ. It must be accepted into "new bottles"—new hearts. That power, that essence of His life, of His fruit bearing, may come into us if we choose, and help us to live the life that He wants us to live, the life that Adam and Eve might have lived.

## The Table of Shewbread

Looking back into the Holy Place of the tabernacle we see at the right the table of shewbread. By its side there were golden containers of wine for drink offerings. These drink offerings were not drunk, they were poured out as oblations by the brazen altar. Now, as far as the points of the compass are concerned, on which side of the tabernacle was the table of shewbread placed? On the north! Take your concordance sometime and study what the Bible says about the "north." Satan's desire was to set his throne "in the sides of the north." He was the first "king of the north." As far as the Bible writers, Jeremiah, Ezekiel, and Isaiah are concerned, north has little to do with geography. Babylon in the king of the north, but it lies eastward. The enemies of Israel came from the north. That was the only way in! The desert road from Babylon was almost impassable for an army to cross the sandy wastes. The people of the east followed the course of the rivers Tigris and Euphrates. They came down through the gates of Damascus into Palestine! The north became identified in the minds of writers of the Bible as the place of the adversary.

When David looked into the Holy Place by faith, he sang, "He set a table before me in the presence of mine enemies, my cup runneth over." So in the tabernacle it was at the north that the table was located. There was the bread and also the wine of "the cup." Where the adversary made his way, there God provided the bread and the wine of the new covenant.

## The Altar of Incense

Next, let us go to the golden altar. The Holy Place is divided up into two squares of ten cubits each. In the center of the more westerly square the golden altar of incense was located, placed diagonally. It had rings in its two edges and rods were used to carry it. It was made all of gold. In the court was an altar of perpetual atonement; in the Holy Place an altar of perpetual intercession. They were connected. They both had horns. The table of shewbread had a crown around the top of it. The mercy seat had a crown around its edge too. A horn is a symbol of power. A crown is an emblem of victory. In the conflicts of life, the two altars provide the essential ingredients—sacrifice and prayer, Calvary and intercession. As far as fellowship is concerned, there is a table of grace and there is the throne of triumph. After the conflict Christ asks us to share with Him the glories of His victory, His crown of life.

On top of the altar of incense a golden bowl was placed. On it live coals, brought from that brazen altar in the court, burned the incense. When was the incense put on these coals? Twice a day, when the morning and evening sacrifices were offered, the incense was presented to the Lord.

## The Daily Service

Let me just review what happened in the daily service in the temple. Before dawn all the priests and Levites who were about to officiate were prepared. They had a bath, they put on clean clothes. The master of ceremonies had decided who was to do what—one was to offer incense, one was to light the candlestick, one was to prepare the morning sacrifice, one was to take away the ashes and prepare the altar—all these tasks had been allocated. One man climbed to the pinnacle of the temple. Remember, Satan took Jesus up there? It was the highest point eastward. Everything was in readiness. The lamb was there at the place of sacrifice. The Levites, who were to fill the laver with their flagons of water, were ready. Other Levites with their load of wood for the altar were prepared—everything was in readiness. The man on the pinnacle was looking eastward for the first ray of the dawning light. The Levite choir was waiting to strike up a song of praise. When the first slanting ray of light climbed over the highlands of Moab and kissed the hills of Hebron, the man on the pinnacle of the temple, cupping his hands, cried down, "It is sanctified!" That was the signal. The priest with the upraised knife slew the victim. The Levites threw open the doors of the temple. The man attending the candlestick fixed the lights. And as Zacharias, the father of John the Baptist, had his turn, the priest was in the Holy Place offering incense.

The Chronicler records that "when the burnt offering began, the song of the Lord began also with trumpets...." (2 Chronicles 29:27) I like to think of that verse. Calvary puts a song in God's heart! Think of that! Do you know what the Hebrews say when they want to think of some important truth? Do you know what David put in the Psalms? "Selah." It means, "Think of it!" When the lamb was slain, the song began and the light shone and the incense rose and all the provision to meet man's sinful need was made in the daily ceremonial. This is the "daily" which Daniel talks about. Every provision was set in operation for another day to help man to victory. On the table was the daily bread. On the golden candlestick was the daily light. In the laver was the daily cleansing. On the altar of atonement was the daily sacrifice. On the altar of prayer was the daily intercession. The priest went daily to the door of the tabernacle and met the penitent, put his arm around him and brought him in, and explained to him what he had to do to gain peace of mind and peace with God. All these things God provided daily. But the little horn took all this away from the Prince of the host. He presented other water, the daily sacrifice of the mass, the church as the only light of the world. There is other bread; the incense is the intercession of saints and angels and Mary. All the "daily" was taken away from Him. But prophecy declared that at the end of the 2300 days, "Then shall the sanctuary be restored to its rightful place." (Daniel 8:14, R.S.V.)*

---

*That is what we are trying to do. That is what Adventists have been doing for more than a century—put the sanctuary, and all it means, back into its rightful place.

Everyday this "daily" service went on. He who by faith came to the priest, followed him in the ministry that was provided in the Holy Place. As Zacharias offered incense, the people outside were praying. The incense was lighted by fire that came from Calvary's altar. That incense was to be made of four ingredients. What are the four ingredients that the Bible says constitute prayer? Praise,—intercession.—Supplication.—Confession. This is the basis of all life. Some of these ingredients are bitter. Some parts of prayer may be bitter. Some parts are fragrant. These thoughts are suggested by the incense.

God has clothed these truths in symbols that we should think about them, and allow their meanings to sink into our hearts. If they help us nearer to the kingdom of God, they have done their job. Would you dogmatize and say that the artist, Harry Anderson, meant only this and this only by his picture, of a small child pointing to the scars on Jesus' hand and asking "What Happened to Your Hand?" Oh, you wouldn't! He means everything you see and maybe a lot more than he himself thought. The sublime illustrations of the plan of salvation embedded in the sanctuary are spermatic. They grow into a fullness of meaning as we meditate prayerfully.

## Growing In Grace

Come by faith into the Holy Place and see the light that shows you the way and eat the bread and drink the cup that gives you strength to grow. Breathe in the atmosphere of prayer-filled incense. This is the atmosphere in which you must walk. You breathe the prayers of Jesus Christ, His merits and intercession. So must prayer be the breath of your soul. Sometimes we think that prayer must be vocal. There are some people who seem to talk all the time they breathe! Prayer is breathing the atmosphere of heaven without necessarily talking. Meditation is allowing the ideas of God to go through our minds. Hold them there in suspension and look at them. Turn around and look at them from another angle, and something will happen to your heart that rush and hurry and restless movement will never achieve. The peace of God will take possession of your soul.

So, the penitent by faith walks in the light, partakes of the bread, breathes the atmosphere and slowly moves westward to the veil that separates him from the Most Holy Place. By faith he can look inside of the Most Holy Place. By faith he can see in the ark a golden pot that had manna. Of what is manna a symbol? Let me read this statement to you from the *Desire of Ages*, p. 386. "It was Christ Himself who had lead the Hebrews through the wilderness and had daily fed them with the bread from heaven. That food was a type of the real bread from heaven. The life-giving Spirit is the true manna." I like that verse in Nehemiah which tells me exactly the same truth. Let me read it to you. Nehemiah, the ninth chapter, verse 20: "Thou gavest also Thy good spirit to instruct them and withheldest not Thy manna from their mouth and gavest them water for their thirst." What is the main characteristic of Hebrew poetry? Someone tell me? Repetition, parallelism—dual or triple. This is triple parallelism, three statements meaning the same thing. "Thou gavest Thy good spirit to instruct them" equals "Thou withheldest not Thy manna from their mouth." These two statements are equivalent to "Thou gavest them water for their thirst." So the spirit is equated with manna and water. Jesus Christ takes that water and He says, If any man thirst, let him come to Me and out of him will flow rivers of living water. This spake He concerning the Spirit. (John 7:37, 38) Mrs. White tells us that manna is a symbol of the Holy Spirit, and so does the Bible.

There are aspects in which Christ may by symbolized by manna, but manna is specifically a type of the Holy Spirit. Where did the manna fall? On the ground, right around the tents of Israel. So, every morning the children of Israel had to make a choice. They had to get down on their knees and gather the manna, or they had to trample on it. We have that choice today with the Holy Spirit, too. We either get down on our knees every morning and gather that manna, or we trample on God's daily provision. What did Israel do with the manna? They could take it home, grind it and make anything they wanted to out of it.* It could be given almost any flavor. The manna would provide for the tastes of everyone. But Israel had to do something about it. They had to gather it. They had to take it home and prepare it. It wasn't ready made. It wasn't predigested.**

---

*The Jews maintain that any kind of flavored food might be made out of manna with one exception. It was something like wheat. You can take wheat and can get the protein out of it and you can make something that will taste like a Choplet or a Chickett! Or you can take it and make it sweet. The manna could not be made it imitate unclean food. That is why the mixed multitude got fed up with it.

**I would recommend that you take your concordance and you get your Bible and make a list of all the texts that deal with manna. There are not many of them.

When Isreal gathered the manna, any roving Bedouin or Edomite could come and share it. But it was given exclusively to Israel. What does Jesus say to us about the Holy Spirit? "I go away. When I go away, I will send Him to you, and when He is come to you, He will convince the world of sin, or righteousness and of judgment." (See John 16:7, 8.) Sin is what we have not got to do, righteousness is what we must do, and judgment is the end of our either doing or not doing! That is what the Holy Spirit is to do. But note that Jesus said, "When He is come to *you*, He will convince the world of sin." Let us never forget the ministry of God is sharing with His remnant people.*

May this illumination of the Holy Spirit, fire us to achieve God's purpose.

---

When did God give manna? When his people did not have any other food. God wanted to test them to see whether they would live by bread only or by every word that cometh from the mouth of God. In their dire need He set a table for them in the wilderness. He never failed. His Holy Spirit will never fail us now.

*The gift of the Spirit is to us. There were many people in Jerusalem on the day of Pentecost, but on whom did the Holy Spirit fall? Only the waiting disciples. They were God's spokesmen. So, in this view not only is there a light for us to walk in, bread for us to eat, an atmosphere in which to journey, but a ministry that we must fulfill as God gives to us His Spirit.

# Study V

## CHERUBIM OF GLORY

### The Ark of the Covenant

Yesterday we thought about the manna in the ark. The ark in the Most Holy Place is the most thrilling and the most profound and the most far-reaching composite symbol in all the tabernacle. The ark was a box made to contain the two tables of the Decalogue. It was of shittim wood, covered inside and out with gold. Josephus tells us that it consisted of three boxes—a box of wood into which was very neatly and tightly fixed a box of gold that fitted it on all four sides and the bottom, and had flanges going over the top edges. Then Bezaleel put that wooden box inside a golden box that went up over the outside so that the wood was completely covered with gold. Part of the edge formed a crown. On top of this ledge the mercy seat was placed. Upon each end of the mercy seat there were cherubim of beaten work. They were not cast in moulds. They were beaten—annealed [to strengthen] and beaten, and annealed and beaten, in hollow work. It took fiery trials and many blows to fit them for this function.

Inside the ark were three* items—the two tables of stone, the golden pot of manna and Aaron's resurrected rod. Aaron's rod was an almond branch that bore buds and blossoms and fruit. In the golden limbs of the seven-branched candlestick this motif was repeated.**

---

*There were three items in the court: The fire, the water and the blood. Justification by faith is taught by the ceremony and symbols in the court.

There were three items in the Holy Place: The lamp, the bread and the incense. Sanctification by faith is set forth in the Holy Place.—The three agencies for attaining sanctification in that Holy Place were walking in light, feasting on the Word, and journeying in the atmosphere of Christ's intercession, suggested by the incense.

There were three items in the ark: The Law, the manna and the rod. Glorification shines from the Most Holy Place.

**Whenever Israel saw that motif they thought of the resurrected rod—the power of God to vindicate His priesthood, to bring life out of a dead stick and to perform the miracles of transforming grace. The living branches of the seven-branched candelabra upheld the light. It is life which uplifts the light.

Ultimately we shall sit with Christ upon His throne. This is symbolized by the mercy seat. Its foundation is Law, manna and the resurrected rod. Only those who have been born again, and made new creatures, will be there. And the food to sustain is spiritual food, it is manna. This is an emblem of the Spirit. As we think about these symbols, how are we ever to attain to the throne of God? Let us remember that side by side with this law, which is so difficult to keep, God has placed an illustration of a resurrection life, and of food which is the Spirit. These will enable us to carry out God's will as we live the life of Jesus empowered by the Spirit of His grace.

## The Rod of God

Moses had cut this rod from a common almond tree, just like other almonds. He had used it in tending his sheep. In Egypt it had become a snake. Then as a cannibal snake it devoured other snakes! Moses had used it to defend himself, to fend off enemies. The rod had helped him in counting the tithe of his flock. it had smitten the gods of Egypt. It had been there at the time of the Red Sea and had parted the way for them. When they had thirsted it had broken open the heart of the Eternal Rock, and the fountain had gushed forth. That rod is called a "rod of God." Finally it had been resurrected.* When the Psalmist looked on the rod he was comforted thereby. There was by the throne this symbol of the resurrection, of the new life that God can work out and maintain miraculously. Here too, His people feed upon the manna that came down from heaven, this emblem of the Eternal Spirit.

## The Law of the Lord

What is this law of God? Law is codified love. Love is the principle of ideal relationships between God the Father, Son and Spirit; between God and angels; between God and unfallen worlds; between God and man; between God and trees; between God and the winds and the waves; between God and the whole solar system, and between man and God and God's creation. For life to continue as the Creator designed, there must be certain ideal relationships. The sun has to remain within its orbit or we would be burned to a crisp. The tides have to stay within bounds.

---

*The Spirit of Prophecy saw it in heaven with the buds and the blossoms and the almonds. (*Early Writings*, p. 32) Sister White tells us that sometimes it was taken out and shown to the people that they might remember.

Nature does not use great cliffs to achieve this but tiny grains of sand. Cliffs wear out, but you never wear out a long sandy beach. It stays there. God's people should remain small and humble too. The Lord likened His people to the sand! They will far better be able to resist floods which the adversary sends against them. Love is the principle that actuates and operates in all these relationships.

What is law? Law is love codified. A young man is growing up into manhood, and, for the first time, he turns his eyes from the east side of the chapel in college to the west. He suddenly discovers that there are interesting persons whom he never noticed Heretofore he has operated by his heels and his elbows. if he wanted to go through a door, he went! Now somebody from the west side wants to get through that door, and for the first time in his life he thinks there might be a more excellent way. Somebody suggests that he make friends with Emily Post. So he gets a book out of the library that tells him what he ought to do when somebody from the west side is going through a door and he is there too. He should open that door and let her through. Well, you say, everyone ought to know that! But sadly there are still some hooligans who haven't realized that they ought to open a door for a lady. Emily Post's book on etiquette is codified courtesy. It makes regulations telling us of what courtesy consists. When you go and get your driver's license, most states give you a little book listing all the rules of the road. There is one rule of considerable importance, I think. You drive on the right hand side of the road, and so everything is safe. The laws of highway etiquette are an extension and application of the commandment, "Thou shalt not kill." The four-way stops, red lights, yielding to the driver on the left—all the regulations of highway courtesy—are illustrations and applications of the principles of the sixth commandment.

As soon as man was created the principle of love encompassed him in all his relationships. God loved. Man operated in the sphere of love. When there was a woman created, that increased the sphere of love's operation. Later man had relationships encompassing his fellow men, the animals, the angels, and his God. God Himself has relationships to man, to angels, to the multiplied orders of creation. When Cain and Abel and Seth and the other members of the family arrived, further regulations, which were extensions of the law of love, were revealed to cover all these relationships.

Now, I don't think a honeymoon couple on their first week back home would need to put rules on the bathroom door like this: "I shall occupy the bathroom from 5:30 to 6:00, and you can come in from 6:00 to 6:30." But when you have 15 people living in the house, you may have to codify love in order to get cooperation and amity everywhere or else the Battle of Armageddon might start right there!

The more relationships spread, the more rules you need. Right rules are illustrations and applications of the principles of love. There are four commandments that show man's relationship to God and God's relationship to man. In the Garden of Eden there was no question of "Thou shalt not commit adultery," because neither Adam nor Eve were the slightest bit interested in such a thing. But when the possibility of sinful relationships came about, then adultery had to be defined. If you really love, you just don't commit adultery. It's so with the laws regarding man's property, and man's reputation.

This codification of love in the tables of the Decalogue was like putting rays of light through a spectrum. Light looks white. When you pass it through a spectrum, you see all the colors of the rainbow. They were all there, all the time, but you didn't see them. So the commandment, "Thou shalt not kill," was there all the time. Although if you like to read in *Thoughts From the Mount of Blessing*, Mrs. White says that when Satan fell it came as a surprise to the angels that there was such a thing as a law. They obeyed it naturally. They loved. There are a few young men who would open a door for their mothers when they were six and seven years of age spontaneously, but most of us have to be taught. So, in our relationships to God and man it is codified love, in the form of regulations and rules, that teaches us how to live aright.

I am often asked the question, "Has health reform anything to do with morality?" Let me read this statement by Mrs. White, "All acts of injustice that tend to shorten life, the spirit of hatred and revenge, indulgence of any passion that leads to injurious acts toward others or causes us even to wish them harm, a selfish neglect of caring for the needy or suffering, all self-indulgence or unnecessary deprivation or excessive labor that tends to injure health—all these are to a greater or less degree violations of the sixth commandment." (*Patriarchs and Prophets*, p. 308)*

---

*This statement is in the chapter on the Ten Commandments. I wish you would read the whole chapter rather than going and looking only for that one declaration. This is an amazing chapter.

Any indulgence or any depriving that injures my health breaks the sixth commandment. So, our health laws are all illustrations and applications of the commandment. "Thou shalt not kill." All enlightened, national laws are applications of the Ten Commandments. Apart from the ceremonial regulations there is only one law. This may be broken down into moral, national, scientific, and health laws—all are illustrations and applications of the basic principle, love.

## Ceremonial Laws

There was only one law until God introduced the ceremonial law at the fall of man. Mrs. White wrote a wonderful series of articles in both the *Signs of the Times* and the *Review and Herald* in 1876. The same articles appeared about two weeks apart in both papers. She emphasizes this twofold system of law. One is codified love, as eternal as God Himself; the other consists of types and ceremonies and ordinances which point to Christ and His ministry. This began at the fall and will end with the completion of the plan of salvation. Now, all the ceremonial law was not nailed to the cross. That may come as a shock! When did the antitype of the day of atonement reach its fulfillment? Yes, in 1844! My, oh my! I was expecting a chorus that would have deafened me! The antitypical day of atonement started on the 22nd day of October 1844. Its ceremonies have been going on ever since. The part of the ceremonial law dealing with Christ's ministry in heaven culminating with Azazel's banishment was not nailed to the cross. When is the antitypical feast of tabernacles? When Christ takes us for a vacation to the new Jerusalem above! When will the jubilee be proclaimed? The jubilee was inaugurated in ancient Israel when the day of atonement services had been completed. They are not yet consummated in reality. The jubilee is yet future.

We see these ceremonial laws spreading over the centuries, showing the details of the plan of salvation in codified form, revealing to us every aspect of the ministry and mediation of Christ the lamb and Christ the priest. The ceremonial law was instituted at Eden and will extend until the new heavens and the new earth are established. Then shall we see their full fruition. But as parts of them, such as the Passover sacrifice and symbol, reached their fulfillment on the cross, they were done away with. The last act of the drama will be the death of Azazel, Then the whole scope of this magnificent system will be complete.

There is therefore a twofold system of law—moral and ceremonial. Let us be careful lest we think that the laws of eating and drinking are ceremonial shadows. Diet regulations have nothing whatever to do with the ceremonial law. Healthful living is enjoined by the sixth commandment.

## New Birth Necessary

So, as the foundation of God's throne, typified by the ark, we see the law—codified love in all its ramifications. Love is the principle of ideal relationships, and law codifies those relationships, sets before us details by which we should operate. Man was created to live that way. But now we cannot live according to the principle of love because the devil has implanted in our hearts the principle of hate. We must be born again. When this occurs the principle of love is once again installed within. Jesus Christ begins to live His life in us, then we love. When we love, we want to know all the details and illustrations of how we may love more fully. Regulations that codify those avenues by which I can show my love to you and my God are in the Decalogue. Right at the basis of the throne of God, the ark, was this codification of love in ideal relationships. The resurrected rod showed the new life that enabled man to live. The pot of manna gave the spiritual meat, that strengthened those who are born to this new life, to continue therein. So the Holy Spirit will supply us with power to live victoriously day by day.

## Cherubim of Glory

Above the mercy seat were cherubim. Who was the first cherub? Lucifer. What does Lucifer mean? "*Confer*," "*defer*," "*ferry*," all come from the Latin word "*fero*" I carry, or I bear. "*Luci*," from "*lux*," means light. So Lucifer signifies "the lightbearer." The function of the original cherub was to spread the light. He was nearest to the Source and was to be the harbinger of the light of the universe. Now, what has Satan become? Prince of darkness! Oh yes, the light went out. He has reversed his status. Instead of bearing the light of God, manifest in Jesus, to the ends of the earth, he has determined to put it out, to spread the sparks of his own kindling—darkness.

What does the word "cherub" mean? Cherub is simply the Hebrew word put into English letters. One book I was reading suggested that the second syllable of cherub probably has the same root as "rabbi" or "rabb." The "k" sound at the beginning indicates "like." "Rabb" means "revered father." It is a title of God. The covering cherub was like God! What did Lucifer say he would become? "Like the Most High." (Isaiah 14:14) We might spend a long time thinking about the Most High. Melchizedek was priest of the Most High. Lucifer said, "I will be like the Most High." Most High means superlative among like things. You don't compare a baby with a camel and say the camel is "most high." You compare a baby with another baby, and a camel with another camel, a mountain with another mountain, and a row of baskets on top of the head of Pharaoh's baker with a row of baskets, and there is one of these like things that is higher than the rest. So, Most High is that revelation of Deity by which He compares Himself with mankind, whose nature He has assumed, and reveals Himself as "the Chiefest among ten thousand and the One altogether lovely." Most High suggests the idea of incarnation. Evidently God had revealed to the angelic concourse that His Son would share His nature with the human race and ultimately exalt men to His throne. Christ was honored before the heavenly universe and Lucifer said, "I am going to be like the Most High." The result was rebellion in heaven and Satan and his followers were thrown out.

Immediately thereafter we see cherubim at the garden of Eden. "The cherubim" is what the Revised Version says. First there was one, then there are two. They are not described in Genesis. Bazaleel was told to make cherubim growing out of the mercy seat. It is not until we come to Ezekiel the first chapter that we get a description of the cherubim—six wings, four faces, human body, calf's legs. man's hands. They are obviously symbols. symbols of the function that Lucifer had in the heavenly courts, and their function was the bearing of light. So, the shekinah, first in the flame of a two-edged sword, and then in the glory that dwelt in the Most Holy Place, shone from beneath the wings of these six-winged cherubim. Each had the face of a man, an ox, a lion and an eagle. You will remember that when I described the camp of Israel we saw on the east side Judah with his emblem, the lion; on the south was Reuben, "Let not his men be few;" on the west side was Ephraim, and Ephraim was "like the firstling of a bull;" and on the north is Dan, and his symbol was a flying eagle. Regal dignity, a lion; communicating sympathy, a man; sacrificial service, an ox; flying vision, an eagle. These are the four major characteristics of our

Lord Jesus Christ. He is a lion, He is the Son of man, He is the greatest sacrifice, and John describes Him as soaring on the wings of an eagle to the throne of God Himself!

So, the likeness of the Most High, like the rays of light through a spectrum, are seen dimly in the cherubim. The cherub has six wings, "with twain he covered his feet, with twain he covered his face, with twain he did fly." The cherubim communicate the will of God upon His sapphire throne in Ezekiel 1, "Through the wheels within wheels." These represent "the complicated play of human events." (*Education*, p. 178) The cherubim controlled events by the help of a "man's hand," and that hand is the hand of the Son of man. This ministry is not blind, it is not mere chance, the "wheels" or the interplay of human events are "full of eyes before and behind." We are full of eyes behind—Our hindsight is always 20/20 vision! But God's purposes are full of eyes before, too. The cherubim are seen again in Revelation 4 and 5, living beings with four faces, wings and eyes about the throne of God. They

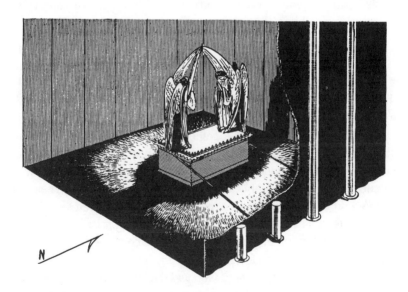

*The Most Holy Place*

sing a new song, a song of victory.

I have several statements by Ellen G. White that I would like to read to you. "Those who walk even as Christ walked, who are patient, gentle, kind, meek and lowly in heart, will see Christ. Heaven will triumph, for the vacancies made in heaven by the fall of Satan and his angels will be filled by the redeemed of the Lord." *(Review and Herald*, May 29, 1900)

"Jesus came to our world to dispute the authority of Satan. He came to restore in man the defaced image of God, to raise him, elevate him, fit him for companionship with the angels of heaven, to take the position in the courts of God which Satan forfeited through rebellion." *(Ibid*, May 8, 1894)

"God created man for His glory. It was His purpose to repopulate heaven with the human race when after a period of test and trial they had proved to be loyal to Him. Adam was to be tested to see whether he would be obedient. Had he stood the test, his thoughts would have been as the thoughts of God, his character would have been molded after the similitude of the divine character." *(Signs of the Times*, May 29, 1901)

"Satan urges before God his accusations, declaring that they have by their sins forfeited the divine protection. He pronounces them just as deserving as himself of the exclusion from the face of God. 'Are these,' he says, 'the people who are to take my place in heaven?' " *(Testimonies*, Vol. 5, p. 473)

"The vacancies made in heaven by the fall of Satan and his angels will be fulfilled by the redeemed of the Lord." *(Patriarches and Prophets,* p. 587)

When I got these thoughts together, I was ready to shout with joy. The service that Satan was to fulfill, of bearing the light of the knowledge of the glory of God to the far-flung unfallen universe, will be carried out ultimately by you and me if we are faithful! We are to be the light bearers of the world now. We are to be "like God, for we shall see Him as He is." (I John 3:1) We can sing a song and bear a testimony that the angels cannot. Through the centuries, since the fall of man, Gabriel has been fulfilling that function next to Christ. He has come to carry the knowledge of God and the knowledge of events yet unfulfilled to those, on the human plane, who can hear and understand the teaching of God. But in the years that have no ending, we will be His witnesses. There, upon the mercy seat, on the foundation of the law of God, sustained by the resurrection life and supported by the manna, the cherubim are the disseminators of light. In the unending ages, that privilege will be ours. What a joy to accompany Christ and His followers to some planet, there to tell the story of redeeming grace, the providences of God that have helped us, to expound the love of God that angels cannot appreciate, and to put into words our praise in language beyond the grasp of even those celestial beings! What a privilege! At the cherubim-guarded gate of paradise this glory was upheld. By faith we look into the Most Holy Place and see this same glory. Oh, that we may be changed into that likeness by His grace!

# Study VI

## BE THOU MADE CLEAN

SIN MAY BE likened to friction in machinery; the more it goes on the more the machinery breaks down. Defilement is the product of that friction or that disharmony in the initial balance of God's creation. We read that God, at the time of the flood, differentiated between clean and unclean creatures. The command given to Noah dealt with a careful, accurate separation between animals that were clean and animals that were not clean. After the flood, the Lord again gives, for the third time, the diet man may eat. Then He added, "But flesh with the life thereof which is the blood thereof shall ye not eat." (Genesis 9:4)

It is practically impossible to eat flesh without blood. The average person who eats flesh breaks this requirement of God. The orthodox Jews are very careful. They kill the animal in a special way, different from the regular method animals are usually killed. When the flesh is cut up into small pieces, the cook soaks it in brine. Thus the particles of blood which are still left are removed. The housewife puts the soaked flesh between toweling and beats it with something like a butter paddle to get all the bloody juices out. By this time you may just as well be chewing rubber! So, the cook gets the spices of Araby, and adds them to the flesh to re-institute flavor. You will recollect that the sons of Eli said they would not eat "sodden" flesh. (I Samuel 2:15) There are lots of sons of Eli who won't eat sodden flesh today! They want the flesh with the blood in it. Fat was prohibited also. It is impossible to get a piece of pork without having fat inside its muscle fiber. I'm not going to enter this morning into a detailed study of this topic, except to give you these insights into these facts. When God says something is unclean, it is unclean! We often compromise, seeking to avoid doing what God has specifically enjoined. But the Lord is not pleased with this attitude toward His expressed commands.

# Uncleanness

There are three kinds of uncleanness spoken of in the Bible, uncleanness connected with issues. These concerned the beginning and end of life and were summed up by the case of the leper. In effect the ceremonies dealing with the cleansing of the leper embraced all the cleansing ceremonies dealing with the defilement of "issues," or exudations from decaying flesh.

Another form of uncleanness concerned the dead. All contact with the dead defiled and so had to be cleansed. The sacrifice of the red heifer and the ritual connected with the application of its purifying virtues covered all cases of "factual" defilement.

The third kind of defilement concerned the basic sinfulness of mankind, which resulted, not from his acts necessarily, though it was aggravated by these, but his innate sinfulness. All the sins of Israel, were, in a sense, stored in the sanctuary. Once each year this type of defilement was removed when the tabernacle was cleansed. The ceremony in which this form of cleansing was depicted revolved around the fate of the two goats.

It is remarkable what a significant part the number three plays in the symbolism of the sanctuary.

You remember that we pointed out that there are three interesting symbols in the court—the fire, the water, and the blood through which justification is brought about. There are three symbols in the Holy Place—the illumination of the lamp, the sustenance of the bread, the atmosphere of the incense—these three teach how sanctification is to be achieved. There are three items in the ark—the law, the manna, and the rod. They provide the foundation for victorious man's ultimate stance in glory. The ark itself consisted of three parts—a box within a box within a box—gold and wood and gold, divinity covering the humanity of Christ. Every board illustrates this point too—gold on each side and wood in the center. The altar exhibited this truth, too—brass and wood and brass. The curtains, the veils, three of them—one to the court, one to the Holy Place, one to the Most Holy Place—all suggest the methods God has provided through Jesus Christ whereby the sinner, out in the camp of Israel, might journey through justification and sanctification to glorification.

But to return to the thought of uncleanness as portrayed in the writings of Moses.

Now, we have three ceremonies to deal with these three kinds of defilement. The one that cleanses from contact with the dead revolves around a red heifer and is described in Numbers 19. The ceremony connected with the issues of every form revolves around the two sparrows offered in connection with the leper and is described in chapters 13 and 14 in the book of Leviticus. The removal of the defilement of sin in its ultimate revolves around two goats and is described in the 16th chapter of Leviticus. Red heifer, two sparrows, two goats, I am always made sad when Christians talk about the sanctuary question and only think of the ceremony of the two goats. What I would like to achieve by this series is to present a balanced picture and then, so interest you, that you will want to go home and study it for yourselves, gathering together all the wonderful statements from the Bible and the writings of the Spirit of Prophecy and anywhere else that you can find them, forming in your heart the thrilling picture of the meaningful symbols that God has presented of the fullness of the ministry of Jesus.

## Red Heifer

Let's find the 19th chapter of Numbers and go through the parts that are relevant. Verse 13 tells us that "Whosoever toucheth the dead body of any man defileth the tabernacle of the Lord." If he does not obtain cleansing, that soul will be cut off. This is the law. When a man dies in a tent, all who come into the tent will be unclean also. Open vessels without a cover will be unclean too. "And whosoever toucheth one that is slain with a sword in the open field or a dead body, or a bone of a man, or a grave, shall be unclean seven days."

For the "unclean person they shall take the ashes of a heifer." We are warned that "some may look upon this slaying of a heifer as a meaningless ceremony, but it was done by the command of God, and there is a deep significance that has not lost its application to the present time." (*Testimonies*, Vol. 4, p. 122) The 9th chapter of Hebrews describes the services of the Day of Atonement. That is why it does not mention a censer or an incense altar in the Holy Place. The reason for this is that the function of the intercession had passed from the Holy Place into the Most Holy Place for that day. Paul concludes in verse 13, "If the blood of bulls and of goats, and the ashes of an heifer sprinkling the unclean, sanctifieth to the purifying of the flesh: How much more shall the blood of Christ, Who through the Eternal Spirit offered Himself without spot, purge your conscience." Paul understood that "the ashes of a heifer" had deep significance for the Christians. We should study it prayerfully.

God declared that the heifer must be red. The Mishna tract that deals with this service is called "Parah." Parah in Hebrew means "heifer." The Jews say that if an otherwise red heifer had two black hairs coming out of one follicle it was not to be considered red! There was a time when the Jews obeyed God! They had light. Salvation was of the Jews. We may learn a great deal from them. When they were looking for a red heifer, they looked for a red heifer! They were extremely careful.

The heifer was not to have been yoked. When Jesus says, "Come unto Me all ye that labor and are heavy laden...take My yoke upon you..." what is that yoke? "The yoke that binds to service is the law of God." (*Desire of Ages*, p. 329) The finest commentary on the red heifer is *Testimonies*, Vol. 4, pp. 120–123. Here we are told that Christ was beyond law. If an angel had come to redeem mankind, he would have been ordered to do so, because he was subject to the law of man. Christ was above law. He made the law. No yoke, no obligation rested upon Him. He came freely, because He could say, "I delight to do Thy will, O God. Yea Thy law is within My heart." (Psalms 40:8)

Moses was to take this red heifer, that was above and beyond all obligation, to the place of death. The prophet asks, who is this that comes with garments dyed red from Bozrah? (Isaiah 63:1) He looks to Christ the antitype of the red heifer. Red is the color of blood. "The life of the flesh is in the blood." Leviticus 17:11. The very color of this heifer was to underline the truth that "in Him was life" (John 1:4) and that His life was being laid down for every man.

When Israel had settled in Palestine they took this heifer to the Mount of Olives. It had to be taken outside the city. On the march this meant outside of the camp. Paul mentions sacrificed bodies that were taken outside the city, and says, "Christ suffered without the gate." This was to teach that He died for the whole world and not for the Jews only. (*Testimonies*, Vol. 4, p. 120) So, this cleansing of the red heifer was to be regarded as universal in its effect. The animal was not to be slain in the court as other sacrifices were. The priest built a pyramid of wood outside. The heifer was led there and washed. It was then backed into an opening in this wooden pyramid. It was thrown as all the sacrifices were thrown. Its two front legs were tied together with a slip knot, which they tightened. It was now standing on its two front legs tied together, and its back legs. Then a slip knot was tied around its back legs, and tightened, until the back legs were pulled to where its front legs were tied. So it fell on its side.

The heifer's face was pointed to the Holy of Holies and its neck was stretched so the whole underside of its throat was taut. I have watched a rabbi take his sharp, ceremonial knife and draw it in one movement across an animal's throat. Then the fountain of blood opens. It splashes against those who are sacrificing it. This elemental ghastliness was to teach that there is nothing pleasant about the death of the Lamb of God. We romanticize Calvary. It was crude and elemental. God died on Calvary in the most shameful of executions!

As the blood was flowing from its veins—and it takes some time to die, it's not pleasant to see, and it's more unpleasant to hear, and it's harrowing to watch—the priest dipped his finger in the blood, and sprinkled it seven times towards the Holy Place. That was the equivalent, symbolically, of the blood's actually being taken into the Holy Place. It was borne, symbolically, on the wings of the wind and carried into the presence of God. When the heifer died, a spark from the brazen altar was applied to this pyramid of wood, and the whole sacrifice was consumed into ashes. While it was burning, the priest was required to add to the pyre, cedar wood, hyssop, and scarlet. The cedar is a token of decay-resisting royalty. It points to the truth expressed in the words, "He did not suffer His Holy One to see corruption." The cedar is the royal tree. Hyssop is a symbol of humility. You remember that Solomon studied natural history from "the cedar that is in Lebanon to the hyssop that springeth out of the wall." The Jews say he loved to meditate upon the service of the red heifer!

Then there was also added scarlet. The Bible uses the word "thread" and the Spirit of Prophecy uses the word "ribbon." It means "a woven piece." This red thread or red ribbon is used first in connection with the birth of Judah's twins. One little boy's hand came out first, and the midwife put a red thread around it. His twin brother actually was born a little before he was! But, because he had put his hand out first, he was a kind of first fruits. So, this red thread marked the firstborn. The next time this word is used it is in connection with the fall of

Jericho. A certain lady had to let out a red thread or red ribbon or cord out of her window. What did that effect in her life? Rahab was spared; she was saved. And, incidentally, she became the ancestress of Christ. It's remarkable that Rahab from Jericho and Ruth from Moab should be adopted into the line of Jesus. They were foreign ladies. It matters not to God where we are born. It matters to God only what we become through grace. So this red thread indicated the firstborn and also marked the submissive for salvation. Whenever Israel saw it, they remembered these stories. Thus the cedar—regal, decay-resisting dignity; hyssop—humility; the red thread—sign of the firstborn, were to be added symbolically to this heifer as it was being burned.

When the ashes had cooled, "indicating a full and complete sacrifice," (*Testimonies*, Vol. 4, p. 121) they were divided into seven parts. One part was placed in each of the six cities of refuge and one part was kept in the tabernacle. All defiled by contact with the dead were to be sprinkled seven times with water from a running stream into which these ashes were mixed, in order to obtain cleansing.

## Defilement By Contact With the Dead

What is meant by defilement through contact with the dead? Paul says, "You hath He quickened who were dead in trespasses and sins." (Ephesians 2:1) We may be walking around and eating three good square meals a day but be actually dead in our trespasses and sins. We may be defiled, too, by contact with those who are thus dead. You work at a desk alongside someone who is dead in trespasses and sins and listen to his jokes every day and listen to his foul language every day. If you are not careful, those words will slip out of your mouth in a moment you are unprepared. If you remain around him long enough, you will think his jokes are funny, too. See! You will be defiled by contact with the dead. People outside Jesus don't dress the way a Christian should dress, and if you aren't careful, if you look at them long enough, you will be defiled by contact with the dead as they are.

Paul describes those dead in sins in the first chapter of Romans. He gives a long list of sin—murder, lying, adultery, pride, vain glory, taking the name of the Lord in vain—you know that terrible catalog of sins—he says in the last verse there are some people, who "knowing the judgment of God, that such things are worthy of death, not only do the same but have pleasure in them that do them!" Do you ever take pleasure in murder? Be careful now! There are some TV plays that have many murders in them. Do you take pleasure in robbery? You may, if you read a book about "who done it." Oh, yes, you can take pleasure in them that do these things! Have you ever looked at a play when the main thought was adultery? Eighty-nine per cent of Hollywood's productions have sex deviations in them. Oh yes, if you're not careful, you can sit and look at that silver screen and take pleasure in those who are doing those things God condemns. You pay for actors to do these acts! And you can listen to songs that are lewd and suggestive. Be careful that you are not defiled by contact with the dead. But if you have been, there is ever open "a fountain for sin and for uncleanliness." The fullness of the sacrifice of Jesus Christ, Who went outside the city walls to find all mankind, with no obligation upon Him, and dies that you might live, will suffice for your need, too.

Water is a symbol too. Jesus said of the Christian, "Out of His belly will flow rivers of living water. This spake He of the Spirit." Paul in discussing the ceremony of the red heifer, says, "so much more shall the blood of Jesus Christ, Who through the eternal Spirit offered Himself, purge your conscience from dead works." There is the ash and there is the water in the type. So there is Christ and there is the Spirit applying to your life the influence of Calvary. The ash and water mixture was to be sprinkled seven times upon the penitent to show that the cleansing was complete.

We read in *Testimonies*, Vol. 4, p. 124 that sometimes there were pious people who had that sprinkling brought right into their homes. They sprinkled their furniture and sprinkled their cooking pots and sprinkled the doors of their houses, and then had an artist put a plaque above the door which read, "I am not my own Lord, I am Thine."*

---

*You know, we ought to have our TV's sprinkled with that water! We ought to have our radios sprinkled with that water! We ought to have our books and magazines sprinkled with that water! We ought to have our cooking pots sprinkled with that water! Our wardrobes ought to be sprinkled, and we should write over the doors of our home, "I am not my own Lord. I am Thine." Thus we would be cleansed from all the defilement which results from contact with those who are dead in their sins.

# The Two Sparrows

Leprosy is a type of sin that erodes and corrodes and discharges poison. When we study the law of the leper, we find that there is a provision made for three kinds of leprosy—leprosy of the body, leprosy of the house, and leprosy of the garment. (Leviticus 13 and 14) Leprosy of the body—the life lived in the flesh; leprosy of the house—our homes; leprosy of garments—our clothes and our righteousness and outward deeds—all these may be leprous. There are some homes that are leprous, and the contagion spreads to the children. There are some clothes that are leprous and hearts are defiled! There are bodies that are leprous, and generations yet unborn are contaminated.

But the leper was not hopeless. He might be cleansed! You remember Jesus told the leper He had healed, "Go shew thyself to the priest and offer for thy cleansing the things that Moses and the law command." He was to bring with him a piece of cedar, scarlet cloth, hyssop, a clean earthenware pot, and two sparrows. He was to come to the court of the sanctuary and there a priest would meet him. Together they would walk out to a living stream and take a scoop of water into his earthen vessel. They would then return to the door of the tabernacle. Here the priest would explain to the cleansed man what the ceremony meant. The leper must stay outside. The priest would step just inside the court. This Mishnaic tract that gives the details of this ceremony is called "Negaim."

The priest at this juncture takes one of the sparrows and pinches off its head, allowing its blood to mingle with the water in the earthen vessel. So now there was a fountain of "water and blood." They had "this treasure in an earthen vessel." "As for the living bird, he shall take it, cedar wood, scarlet, hyssop and dip them and the living bird in the blood of the bird that was killed over the running water." (Leviticus 14:5) The priest next took the short cedar branch the leper had brought, and tied the hyssop on to the cedar with the scarlet cloth or ribbon, like a corn stalk broom. He dipped this hyssop into the water and blood and sprinkled the leper seven times. Now he let the living bird loose in an open field after he had dipped it in the water and blood. Listen to this remarkable insight into this ceremony: "The wonderful symbol of the living bird, dipped into the blood of the slain bird and then set free to its joyous life, is to us the symbol of the atonement. There death and life are blended, presenting to the searcher of truth the hidden treasure, the union of the pardoning blood with the resurrection and life of our Redeemer. The bird was slain over the living water and that flowing stream was a symbol of the ever-flowing, ever cleansing efficacy of the blood of Jesus Christ." (*Sons and Daughters of God*, p. 226)

After Christ died, He, too, arose up into the open heavens. The leper brought two sparrows. When the poor little bird was killed it fell to the ground. A farthing was one of the smallest coins. Christ was trying to show that the plan of salvation costs man very little, but entailed the death of the sacrifice when He said, "Are not two sparrows sold for a farthing? And one of them shall not fall to the ground without your Father." (Matthew 10:29) You know, the gospel is wrapped up in the life story of the homely brown sparrow! Where does a sparrow like to live? Under the roof of our homes. So Christ came and pitched His tent alongside of the tents of men. What food does a sparrow like to eat? The crumbs that fall from the master's table. So Christ came, lived among men and died to carry into the highest heavens the redemption that His blood had purchased!

All this was done for the leper. He was shaved and sprinkled, On the seventh day he came to the door of the court. This time he brought a sacrificial animal and oil. As he stood outside, the outer veil was uplifted. Inside the court was the priest and inside the road to glorification, but he was still outside. The priest said to him in effect, "Put your head over the line." And so over the line that marked the court from the camp, he put his head. The priest took some blood from the sacrifice the leper had brought and anointed his right ear. Then the leper stepped back. The priest said again, "Put in your hand." He put in his right hand and the priest anointed his thumb. He drew it back. The priest said, "Put in your right foot." As he put in his right foot, the priest anointed his big toe. What do you do with your ears? Hear! Whom? Christ. Our ears must be anointed. What do you do with your right hand? Work! What do you do with your feet? Walk! So our hearing, our working and our walking must be anointed with Calvary's blood. Then the priest put some of the oil where the blood had been placed on the leper's ear, hand, and foot. Oil symbolizes what? The Holy Spirit. We must be anointed both by the blood of Christ and the oil of the Spirit! Then, and only then, the road to triumph was open to the leper.

## The Two Goats

The third ceremony dealing with defilement revolved around two goats. It was the yearly service of the tabernacle. Its purpose was to remove sin from the camp of Israel. It occurred on the tenth day of the seventh month, and was called the Day of Atonement, or the Day of Judgment. It is now called "Yom Kippur" by the Jews. On this day the climax of all the ceremonies of Israel reached their focus. The high priest alone carried out the services. He did not sleep the night before. He reviewed all his tasks. At dawn he washed himself, and washed all the sacrificial animals that were to be offered that day, examining their skin square inch by square inch, in case during the night a pimple developed. It would have had a "spot" and so could not be used! When he was satisfied that the animals were absolutely without blemish, he approached the morning sacrifice and waited for the herald of that day to shout, "It is sanctified." He then slew the animal and offered the morning sacrifice with all its intricate details. It took him perhaps two hours to cut and skin and dissect and offer it on the altar, washing its parts. He would then carry out the regular duties of the day, preparing the seven-branched candlestick by taking out the old wick with the snuffers, removing the ash, and putting fresh oil in. He sparked the lamps with a coal from the altar of sacrifice. He would next offer incense on the golden altar. Then he would wash himself, lay aside his pontifical robes and put on the white robes of a common priest.

Coming into the court, he would find a bullock waiting for him. "Aaron shall come into the Holy Place with a bullock, and he shall put on the holy linen coat, linen breeches, girded with a linen girdle mitre on his head; therefore, shall he wash his flesh and so put them on." (Leviticus 16:4). He slew this bullock "for himself and for his house." Taking up a censer with coals from the brazen altar and a handful of incense he went through the Holy Place towards the northern end of the veil which separated the holy from the Most Holy Place. With his elbow he opened the veil and, perhaps for the first time in his life, he found himself in the Most Holy Place. With his back to the veil, he edged sideways along the veil until he was in front of the ark. Then he stepped over the rod with which the ark was carried until he stood between the two rods, the ends of which were out in the Holy Place.

Stepping towards the ark, he put the censer on the floor, poured the incense on the coals, and immediately the Most Holy Place was filled with the fragrance of incense. Then, backing up until he felt the veil, he edged to its southern end. He must never turn his back to the ark. It was too sacred. Then he went out into the court and washed his hands and his feet at the laver. Picking up the golden bowl containing the bullock's blood that one of his helpers had been stirring to prevent it from coagulating, he went back into the Most Holy Place. He goes to the northern end of the veil as before, opens it and stands between the veil and the mercy seat with the fragrant incense now rising before him. Dipping his finger into the blood he smears it on the mercy seat. So the high priest fearfully enters the presence of God with incense and blood.*

Having sprinkled the bullock's blood on the ark the high priest returned to the court. He took the goat's blood, after he had slain the one on which the Lord's lot fell, and entered the Most Holy Place for the third time. Where he had presented the bullock's blood, he offered the goat's blood. He came into the Holy Place and mixed the goat and bullock's blood in front of the golden altar. Then he sprinkled the altar and the veil with the mixture of the blood. You can read the details in the Mishnaic tractate "Yoma." So the high priest had been in the Most Holy Place three times, with incense, the blood of the bullock, and the blood of the goat, up to this point in the ritual.

Entering the court again he carried out the ceremony connected with Azazel. This part of the ritual we know. Azazel was banished to the wilderness bearing the guilt of which he was guilty. After he offered the evening sacrifice, the high priest went in to the Most Holy

---

*In the 5th chapter of Hebrews, Paul, describing the work of the high priest, summarizes, "So also Christ..." Most commentators declare that the bullock's blood was offered by the high priest because he was the sinner. But he had already offered the morning sacrifice. Had he been still sinful, like Nadab and Abihu, he would have been destroyed before he entered the Most Holy Place. This offering of the bullock's blood is very significant. I submit for your meditation that Christ first presented His petition to His Father. This is symbolized by the incense which the high priest first took into the Most Holy Place. Our Lord's intercessory prayer is recorded in the seventeenth chapter of John. Then, before He could minister on behalf of His people, as He in effect told Mary on the resurrection morning, "I must first be endorsed by My Father," (See John 20:17.) He ascended to God and was accepted as man's representative. So with intercession and blood Christ was established as the Advocate for God's people.

Place for the fourth time. He picked up the censer of incense that had been smoking all day and brought it into the Holy Place, with the result that "the whole house was full of smoke." Remember Revelation 15:8? Then he took the censer outside. This meant that intercession had ceased and probation had closed. Then the trumpet was sounded to inaugurate the jubilee and the people were free!

In this ritual of the two goats, the completion, the climax of all the ceremonies of the plan of salvation, was reached. Azazel is a symbol of the devil. When the whole work had been completed in type, the guilt was laid upon him. We use the word "bear" to describe Azazel's part. He was to "bear" the guilt into the wilderness. We say too, "Christ bore our sins." The words are used accurately. But the connotation we place on each is different.*

Why is it that the guilt is put upon Azazel or Satan? The reason may be simply illustrated something like this: This auditorium may grow very warm. I ask one of the ushers to open a window. He takes a pole to push it up. As he is passing a foot darts out, a mischievous foot, and he is tripped. He plunges the end of the rod through the window and it is broken! Who broke the window? Why, we all saw that the usher broke the window, of course! But we did not see that darting foot. So, with the sinner, we see him sin, but we do not always see the foot that has tripped him. The tempter must be exposed to the universe, when all his work is completed. Oh, yes, we've all sinned! We must die! But Christ died for us, for everyone. He does not only bear the sins of the righteous. Christ has borne every sin of every man that ever came into the world. The purpose of the ceremony with Azazel is to point out to the universe that Satan is the instigator of all sin.

When the millennium is complete, if we are inside the city of God we shall see outside those who are lost. We shall see them gritting their teeth and wanting to drag Christ from His rainbow-arched throne. Then we shall say without any questioning, "Just and true are Thy ways, Thou King of saints." (Revelation 15:3) Even if tears run down our faces in anguish at the loss of loved ones we shall know God's

---

*Unless he is careful, the superficial reader may think that we make Azazel our sin-bearer. But that is silly! "Without the shedding of blood there is no remission of sins." Azazel never died in the ritual! "The wages of sin is death." Azazel did not die. In the wilderness he was to prefigure Satan during the millennium. For a thousand years Satan will be in a land not inhabited. The universe will look down and say, "Is this the man that made the earth to tremble?" Isaiah 14:16.

ways are right. The promise is that at that time God will wipe away all tears from off all faces. If my little daughter is outside, it will take God to dry the fountain of my tears. Won't it be so with you? That is why the story in Revelation is put the way it is!

We see in these services of cleansing the complete method by which God proposes to remove guilt. This is the profoundest transaction, the most thrilling event, in the history of the universe.

"The typical day of Atonement was a day when all Israel afflicted their souls before God, confessed their sins, and came before the Lord with contrition of soul, remorse for their sins, genuine repentance and living faith in the atoning sacrifice."—*Review and Herald*, Dec. 16, 1884.

"As Jesus moved out of the Most Holy Place, I heard the tinkling of the bells upon His garment, and as He left, a cloud of darkness covered the inhabitants of the earth. There was then no mediator between guilty man, and an offended God. While Jesus had been standing between God and guilty man, a restraint was upon the people; but when Jesus stepped out from between man and the Father, the restraint was removed, and Satan had the control of man. It was impossible for the plagues to be poured out while Jesus officiated in the Sanctuary; but as His work there is finished, as His intercession closes, there is nothing to stay the wrath of God, and it breaks with fury upon the shelterless head of the guilty sinner, who has slighted salvation and hated reproof. The saints in that fearful time, after the close of Jesus' mediation, were living in the sight of a holy God, without an intercessor. Every case was decided, every jewel numbered.... Then I saw Jesus lay off His priestly attire, and clothe Himself with His most kingly robes—upon His head were many crowns, a crown within a crown—and surrounded by the angelic, He left heaven."—*Spirit of the Prophecy*, Vol. 1, pp. 198, 199.

"The time is right upon us when there will be sorrow in the world that no human balm can heal. The Spirit of God is being withdrawn from the world. Disasters by sea and land follow one another in quick succession. How frequently we hear of earthquakes and tornadoes, of destruction by fire and flood, with great loss of life and property. Apparently these calamities are capricious outbreaks of seemingly disorganized, unregulated forces, but in them God's purpose may be read. They are one of the means by which He seeks to arouse men and women to a sense of their danger." —*Review and Herald* Feb. 26, 1914.

May God help us to study these symbols so as to understand His love more fully.

# Study VII

## FESTIVALS OF JOY

MANY CHERISH A BOOK by J.N. Andrews, which was revised by Conradi, called *The History of the Sabbath*. Almost in every chapter there is a footnote referring to the works of Robert Cox. In 1865 Robert Cox published two volumes titled *The Literature of the Sabbath Question*. He collected every text in the Bible that deals with the Sabbath, either directly or indirectly; adding every statement that Philo, Josephus, and the other Jewish fathers wrote, and included the church fathers, Catholic and Greek, adding every declaration by Protestant writers until the date of publication. It is a monumental and magnificent work! Regarding questions you have on most statements men have made on the Sabbath, you can find answers in *The Literature of the Sabbath Question*.

While in Edinburgh I made the discovery that Robert Cox presented to the National Library of Scotland, in a special Cox bequest, all his books and tracts on the Sabbath. One day I thought I'd ask the librarian, "Where is the Cox Bequest housed?" She looked quizzical and said, "I don't know! Nobody has ever asked me that question before. I'll go and see." She came back in a minute or two with a bunch of keys and took me upstairs to a vaulted room, overlooking Advocates Close in the ancient city of Edinburgh under the shadow of St. Giles Cathedral. Just across the road is the Church of the Covenanters where some ancient Christians signed the covenant to be faithful to God, with their blood. I stood in a room about 20 feet in diameter. From floor to ceiling, were shelves of books gathered from the ends of Europe by this Presbyterian lawyer and antiquarian, Robert Cox. He never kept the Sabbath though his hobby was collecting everything written on the Sabbath! There were handwritten pamphlets written in the 8th and 9th centuries that he had dug out of libraries and monasteries in Europe; incunabulae, books published before the invention of printing; and then all published books he could lay his hands on—thousands of works. His *Literature of the Sabbath Question* is a bibliography on a vast scale. In a secondhand book store in Edinburgh was found a bound volume of pamphlets. On its title page was, "The

Works of Pope." Inside this book was a tract called, *Septenary Institutions*. It was anonymous. I read it through and thought, "The style sounds just like Cox." I asked the librarian and she said, "It is attributed to Robert Cox." I replied, "I thought so." What I am about to tell you, I got out of that book by Cox, one of the greatest authorities on the Sabbath.

## The Meaning of the Word Sabbath

Cox was interested in the etymology of the word "Sabbath." As I have said before, I believe the Holy Spirit has put his hand over certain words in the Bible that are not translated. What does Sabbath mean? This is what Robert Cox suggests: The word "Sabbath" consists of six letters in transliteration but only three in Hebrew. Cox divides this into two parts. He suggests that Sabbath consists of "Sab" and "Bath." The root of "Sab" is "Ab." "Ab" we find in the English words "abbott" and "abbey." In Paul's writing we see that "abba" means father. Put an "s" in front of it, and you get "sab." How many of you have been to India? Who is "sab?" A master, a learned man. "Sab" or "sahib" means "respected sir," "revered sir," "learned sir," or "learned father." That is what Robert Cox suggests is the significance of "Sab" in Sabbath.

Now the "ath" at the end of Sabbath may have been the original pronunciation or it may have been modified to "oth," Cox suggests. If you will look up Strong's Concordance, you will find that this word "oth" means "sign." I go down the street looking for a red and white striped spiral rod. What am I looking for? A barber's shop! If you saw "R$_x$," what would you think of? A drug store! The Hebrew word "ath" designates a symbol of some profession or place. When the Hebrews put a "b" in front of it, they changed the vowel to "eth." For example, "Bethlehem." What does this mean? "House of Bread" or "home of the baker." That is where the Bread of Life came into the world, so it was a perfectly appropriate name for the birthplace of Jesus! Other names were Bethabara, Bethphage, and Bethel. The prefix "B" indicates the home or dwelling place or the resting place designated by the sign or mark. So Sabbath, Cox suggests, indicates the resting place of the everlasting Father and is His sign. When I first read Cox's suggestion and remembered that the Sabbath is a "sign between Me and you throughout your generations," thought that this was possibly one reason why the Spirit of God had not allowed the translators to render the Hebrew word into English. To translate Sabbath as rest would indicate what the Sabbath is intended to do and not what the word means.

The Sabbath pervaded all Hebrew reckonings of time. The Sabbath has been observed from the beginning. Yet the question is often asked, "Can it be proven that the Sabbath falls on Saturday?" The Jews have kept it without a break for at least three thousand years. The Christian Church has kept Easter Sunday, which is the first day of the week, nearly two thousand years. So the weekly cycle has never been interrupted. *Webster's Unabridged Dictionary* or the *Encyclopedia Britannica* will clarify this. God organized Hebrew annual reckonings on the basis of the Sabbath.

### MONTHS OF THE YEAR

| 1 | 2 | 3 | 4 | 5 | 6 | 7 | 8 | 9 | 10 | 11 | 12 | 1 | 2 | 3 | 4 | 5 | 6 | 7 | 8 | 9 | 10 |
|---|---|---|---|---|---|---|---|---|---|---|---|---|---|---|---|---|---|---|---|---|---|
| 1 | 2 | 3 | 4 | 5 | 6 | ⑦ | ←C | | | | | 1 | 2 | 3 | 4 | 5 | 6 | ⑦ | ← | | |
| ⑦ | ←S | | | | | 1 | 2 | 3 | 4 | 5 | 6 | ⑦ | ← | | | | | 1 | 2 | 3 | 4 |

These squares are months in the sacred year and civil years. "S" indicates sacred and "C" civil. The year generally had twelve months. It may have had thirteen on occasion. The two kinds of years ran side by side. The first month of the sacred year was the seventh month of the civil year. The seventh month of the civil year, in turn was the first of the sacred year. So seven interlocked in the Hebrew reckoning of time.

## Passover

The first sacred month was important because on the tenth day the Paschal lamb was set aside, to be slain on the 14th. Jesus Christ was condemned to die by the Sanhedrin four days before the crucifixion on the tenth day. "These types were fulfilled, not only as to events, but as to time." *(Great Controversy, p. 399)* Having set the Lamb of God apart the Jewish people awaited only an opportunity to put Him to death. Following the triumphal entry on Palm Sunday after the sun was set, He was condemned to death. On the 10th day the Lamb of God was set aside.

On the 14th day the Passover lamb was to be slain. From the 15th for a week, the feast of unleavened bread was celebrated. On the 16th the Wave Sheaf was presented before the Lord. All this took place in the first religious month (which was the seventh civil month, Exodus 13:1, 2) and pointed to Jesus Christ. He was condemned on the 10th, died on the 14th, rested in the grave on the 15th, rose again, as the Wave Sheaf, on the 16th as a kind of first fruits and as a guaranty of the great harvest that will be gathered into heaven at the end of the world.

Let us study the Passover. The unleavened bread meant freedom from sin. Jesus says, "Beware of the leaven of the Pharisees, which is hypocrisy!" (Matthew 16:6) The Pharisees believed in righteousness by works. They were hypocrites. They had two standards. One standard they gave their children, or tried to, and the other standard they failed to live up to themselves. Let us beware of having two standards. We often tend to think that our own weaknesses are not that serious.— this is Phariseeism. "Beware of the leaven of the...Sadducees" (Matthew 16:6), which is materialism. The Sadducees did not believe in the supernatural nor in the afterlife. They were materialists. This life was all that mattered. Beware of that philosophy. "Beware of the...leaven of Herod" (Mark 8:15), which is politics. Herod was an Edomite, descended from Esau. He was no Jew, but a temporizing politician who waded to the throne through blood. He believed in power as a creed. Beware of the leaven of Herod. All leaven must be removed before the children of Israel could cross the Red Sea and turn their faces toward Canaan.

The Paschal lamb was to be eaten roasted. John Eadie (a religious author in the mid-1800s) explains how Jews roasted this lamb. They passed a rod from its throat to its vent so that it would be rotated as we do on a pit barbecue. They spread out its chest cavity with another stick at right angles to that rod. Thus for 1500 years the paschal sacrifice had been spitted on a cross of wood! Without a bone broken, "crucified," the lamb was prepared to be eaten with bitter herbs. There were endive and similar greens. Unleavened bread, endive, the lamb, and then the cup of wine, these were partaken of at the Passover. Since the Passover occurred in March, there are no grapes. Grapes ripen in August. To obtain unfermented wine they reconstituted raisins. We did the same for our Communion Service during the war. Water, the emblem of the Holy Spirit, brings out again the juice of the dried grapes, symbol of the new covenant in His blood. And so Israel ate the Egyptian Passover with their loins girt and their clothes on, ready to go. But in the Jerusalem Passover, they ate it reclining. This was to suggest that they had now ended their pilgrim way, and were now at rest.

## Pentecost

What were the Hebrews to count from the 16th day of the first month? Seven Sabbaths. (Leviticus 23:15, 16) They had a Sabbath of weeks. As we have already seen in the interlocking seven month periods each year they had months in which to remember the Sabbath. Then from the 16th day of the first sacred month, which was the day of the resurrection, they were to count seven Sabbaths. On the morrow following the seventh Sabbath, fifty days, Pentecost occurred. Paul tells us that when Israel left Egypt "They were all baptized into Moses in the cloud and in the sea." (I Corinthians 10:4) The Red Sea was a type of baptism. Baptism is a symbol of the burial of Christ. On the 16th day after the Passover in Egypt, the Hebrews came out of that watery grave on their way to Canaan. Fifty days after that they stood at the foot of Sinai. On Sabbath the Father and Son came down on the Mount. Side by side, Father and Son, on the fifteenth day, proclaimed the law. Ever after Israel was to remember what happened on that first Pentecost.

At Pentecost two wheat loaves were offered. As we have noted Pentecost not only commemorated the giving of the law on Sinai, it also looked forward to the giving of the Spirit in fullness. The Passover not only commemorated the escape from Egypt, it also looked forward to Christ the Passover who would die for the world.

## New Moons

Every month had a new moon festival marking the first day. This new moon festival on the seventh month had special ceremonies. Each month, as the new moon was sighted, the priest took the trumpet and sounded a blast. On the Mount of Olives he would light a fire, and all over Palestine these would be strategically placed on mountain tops. When they saw that flame, they would know the new month had been sanctified. The day that followed, new month day (month is but a corruption of moonth) the people had a holiday.

New moon day was especially a festival for women. If they wished to have a Bible study they might visit the prophet. (II Kings 4:23) The Sabbath and the new moon are two festivals we shall observe in the New Earth. (Isaiah 66:23) Each "New Moonth" day we shall go up to Jerusalem to eat the new fruit from the Tree of Life. (Revelation 22:1) The purpose of that fruit is for the healing of the nations. Then "there will be no more curse." Every month God provided a day in which the women could look forward to the time when the curse would be over. The healing power for the life cycle of humanity will be restored in the new heavens and the new earth. Every month in this festival the mystic church (symbolized by a virtuous woman) was to look forward to the time of her complete restoration.

## Feast of Trumpets

The seventh New Moon festival on the first day of the civil year is called the Feast of Trumpets. On that day, not only were lamps lighted but everyone got a trumpet or shell or ram's horn. When the priest sounded the silver trumpet in the sanctuary, everyone sounded his trumpet, too, because later on the tenth day, would fall the Day of Atonement and all must get ready.

## Day Of Atonement

The Day of Atonement is the Day of Judgment to the Jewish people. Then the souls of all man will come up before Jehovah. On the tenth day they were to set a trumpet to every lip. Joel tells us to sound an alarm because the day of judgment is near, "the day of the Lord is near and hasteth greatly." It is remarkable that in 1833 William Miller received his license to preach. For ten years thereafter he proclaimed that the judgment was coming and that the end of the world was near. While he missed his calculation, on the tenth day of the seventh month—22nd of October 1844 as we know it—the judgment began in the Day of Atonement services, in the heavenly sanctuary.

In the first sacred month, the lamb was set aside on the tenth day. In the seventh sacred month, the Lamb in the midst of the throne (Revelation 5:6) provided His blood for the cleansing of every sinner. On the 14th day of the first month the angel passed over those who were covered with the blood; in the seventh month the angel of mercy will spare those who are covered by this blood.

# FEASTS OF JEHOVAH
## Leviticus 23

**SPRING**

| Passover | Unleavened Bread | Wave Sheaf | Pentecost |
|----------|------------------|------------|-----------|
| * | * | * | * * |

| Crucifixion | Communion | Resurrection | Holy Spirt |
|-------------|-----------|--------------|------------|
| FRIDAY | SABBATH | SUNDAY | SUNDAY |

**AUTUMN**

| Trumpets | Day of Atonement | Tabernacles |
|----------|------------------|-------------|
| * | * | * * |

| 1st Angel | Judgement | New Earth |
|-----------|-----------|-----------|
| 1833 | 1844 | —— |

## Feast of Tabernacles

In the seventh month there was also a week of festival, just as there was in the first month. The Feast of Unleavened Bread corresponds to the Feast of Tabernacles. For one week the children of Israel left their homes and lived in booths. They generally made their shelters out of palm leaves. In Mexico and other countries they still make shelters and walls of leaves. For one week Israel was to remember that life on earth was a pilgrimage. The Feast of Tabernacles has not yet met its fulfillment. In 1844 the Day of Atonement reached its antitype. Ever since the work of judgment has been going on. When this is complete the real feast of tabernacles will occur. For the feast of tabernacles on earth, the children of Israel were required to journey to Jerusalem. When the real feast of tabernacles takes place, we shall journey to the new Jerusalem. There we shall live in a temporary abode until the new heavens and new earth are created and every man inherits his possession.

On the last day of the feast of tabernacles, known as "the great day," (John 7:37) occurred a special ceremony. When the children of Israel were in the wilderness, the priest went out to the water gushing from the smitten rock. In Jerusalem they descended from Mt. Moriah or Zion, into the narrow valley below, and found their way to the pool of Siloam. The priests dipped their pitchers into it and "with joy gathered water from the wells of salvation." Putting the pitchers on their shoulders they ascended the slopes of Moriah, with Olivet on one side and the Kidron trickling at their feet.* The priest went ten paces and paused and the Levite choirs joined in a song of joyful praise and exultation for the River of Life that was flowing for the benefit of Israel. Then the priest took ten more steps, and again there was another stanza. So the priests made their way with slow dignity till they entered the temple gates into the courtyard. They moved ten paces at a time until they stood at the east of the great altar. There stood two lily-shaped funnels, made of gold. Into one a priest poured water; into the other he poured wine. The water and the wine "flowed mingling down" under the altar, and joined in a stream that went down into the Kedron, and so on into the Dead Sea.**

---

*Read *Desire of Ages*, on the Feast of Tabernacles, pp. 447–454. It is the most magnificent description of the ceremony available.)

**In 1957 we went underneath where that altar had stood, beneath the Dome of the Rock. I said to myself, "I wonder whether those openings are there?" Sure enough,

The Dead Sea is a symbol of "people and multitudes and nations and languages, "that are "dead in their trespasses and sins." The life-giving stream is to go thither as Ezekiel chapter 47 describes. Wherever it goes, the water, or peoples, are healed.

Jesus watched for a while as the priests were coming in and pouring the water on the "last day, the great day of the feast" (John 7:37). At last He moved to a raised portico and called out, with a loud voice, to the millions assembled before Him, "Come unto Me" (John 7:37). Jesus stood there and called out on that last day, that great day of the feast, "If any man thirst, let him come unto Me and drink" (John 7:37). He was the smitten rock. It was from His heart the cleansing stream was to flow. Some few came!*

In the evening, to the right and to the left of the entry way into the magnificent temple two great torches were lighted and the whole temple area illuminated. The light blazed over into the Mount of Olive's brow a quarter of a mile away. That evening Jesus said, "I am the Light of the world" (John 8:12), not those symbols in the temple but He Himself was the true Light. Those lamps had commemorated the pillar of fire that had illumined Israel in days gone by. They were an emblem of Israel, too. That is why pious Hebrews today have the seven-branched candlestick in every home. But you know, Jesus said in effect when He wrote to the church, made up mainly of converted Jews in the first century, If you do not love, if you do not live…, the candlestick will go out; it will be taken away. (Revelation 2:5) One day the armies of Titus rode up from the Dead Sea along the Jericho road. They cantered into the valley of the Kidron and scaled the walls

---

they were there! The Moslem guide said, "When the temple of Solomon was built here, these openings are where the blood, wine, and water flowed down." This twin stream of water and blood, or water and wine, for the wine symbolizes blood, went on to the Dead Sea.

*Josephus tells us that the Passover and other feasts in the time of Christ were attended by three-and-a-half million souls. The Jews record that they killed as many as 250,000 lambs in one Passover! Jesus stood there with the multitudes milling around. They had come from the North and the South and the East and the West, a few from this village, more from that other town. And as they entered those pilgrim ways, they would sing the songs of Zion. The multitudes, coming out of the hills would hear that song and join them. At eventime, 3,500,000 people would take up the well known choruses of Israel of old and singsongs of praise to Jehovah. Can you picture that? 3,400,000 people, singing the great hallel that David had written a thousand years before!

and put out the light of Israel. The candle was extinguished. The heritage was removed. The kingdom was taken away and given to another people bringing forth fruits in righteousness.

## The Sabbath—Sign of the Creator

And so, in this sweep of the recording of time for a year, we see interlocking Sabbaths. We see every fourth week the Feast of New Moon. We see in the first and seventh month twin ceremonies, Passover and Tabernacles, the beginning, the climax, the starting out on the road when the firstborn was saved to the harvest home and the Feast of Tabernacles. Not only was there a Pentecost of days, but there was a Pentecost of years, and the jubilee took place every fifty years. Not only was there a Sabbath of days and a Sabbath of weeks and a Sabbath of months, but there was a Sabbath of years. Every seventh year was the Sabbatical year.

Have you ever tried to figure out how much time Israel was required to spend in worship? Every seventh day, every new moon. All the men had to travel to Jerusalem three times a year; and the women could if they wished. What would happen if you lived 100 miles away and you had to walk the distance or go on a donkey? It would take you three days to get there and three days to get back, and the festival lasted eight, so you spent three weeks at the Passover. You spent more than three weeks at the Day of Atonement and Tabernacles. If you wanted to go for Pentecost—you will remember that Paul says, "I am hurrying that I may get to Jerusalem by Pentecost." you spend more time! An Israelite devoted a month or more just on festivals, maybe two months if he lived far away! Then, every seventh year they were not to do any work. They were to study the Scriptures. When the fiftieth year came, not only did they have the seventh of the last cycle, but they also had the fiftieth, so there were two years in which they were not to work. What did they have to do then? God prescribes it. They should study the law.*

---

*There are some folk who can't afford to spend time to come for ten days to a camp meeting to study. They are too busy! They've got time for golf and boating, but to study? No! Israel did exactly the same thing. They quit coming to the sanctuary after a while. You read in Lamentations 1:4, "The ways of Zion do mourn because none come to the solemn feasts." Israel's knowledge of all these things died.

We do not maintain knowledge without effort. If I know something vividly today, if I'm not careful, in a year from now I will know only a tenth of it. If I don't think about it anymore, in two or three years I won't remember anything about it. Knowledge doesn't remain. You've got to keep up with it all the time. So Israel left out of their thinking all this interlocking movement of the seventh day, the seventh week, the seventh month, the seventh year, the Pentecost of days, the Pentecost of years—left them all out. Materialism took hold of them and the leaven of the Sadducees came into their lives and they perished.

The Lord warned us that the people would say, "What are we going to do about dangers, and robbers and poverty?" And He promised, "Thrice in the year shall all your men children appear before the Lord God, the God of Israel. For I will cast out the nations before thee, and enlarge thy borders: neither shall any man desire thy land, when thou shalt go up to appear before the Lord thy God thrice in the year." (Exodus 34:23, 24)

One day very soon the work of the tenth day of the seventh month will be finished and the trumpet of jubilee will sound. Paul says, "The trumpet shall sound, and the dead shall be raised incorruptible, and we shall be changed. For this corruptible must put on incorruption, and this mortal must put on immortality." (I Corinthians 15:52, 53) Great chariots of fire will sweep us from this earth through corridors of illimitable space, and we shall stand at last before the throne of God in that new heaven and that new earth. This is our home. For a thousand years we shall spend a vacation with Jesus, living with Him. There is plenty of room "in My Father's house," (John 14:2) Jesus promised. He has made perfect provision for all of us.

In all this teaching concerning time, God was trying to push the minds of Israel forward, forward. Time is lent to us to prepare for something that is ahead. In the sacrificial system, the atonement of Christ is depicted. In the mediation of the priest and his life of service, the intercession of Christ is portrayed. In all the ceremonies connected with time, our relationship to eternity is suggested. Oh, may the Spirit of God come upon us to help us to study that we may become cognizant of the light that is streaming to us from the Bible.

# Conclusion

We have come to the end of this series of seven meditations upon the symbolism of Jesus Christ and His ministry, and of the church and of the human soul. God's purposes are here revealed symbolically, pictorially, so that as we observe, though there may be no voice, no language, they may speak to us the language of Canaan. One thing I have tried to do—to reveal Jesus portrayed in these types and ceremonies. Now, I make one request of you, that you will "study to show yourself approved of God," that you will take your Bible and read it. Get all the passages relative to some theme. Quietly, as you are thinking each morning, or during the day, or when you're driving your automobile, let these ideas go through your mind. I can promise you that the Bible will be the most interesting, the most thrilling, the most inspiring, the most Christ-revealing Book that you have ever encountered. How much time should you spend? Fifteen minutes a day will amaze you. You could read the Bible through easily in a year spending fifteen minutes a day. The Holy Spirit will help you. Jesus will manifest Himself to you. I am wondering whether there are any who will be ready to covenant with me, that, by the grace of God, we will spend a minimum of 15 minutes a day, studying our Bibles? Do not do it if you think you are not going to, but if you think you would like to do it by God's help, will you stand with me before the throne. God bless you all. I can promise that you are going to see a change in your lives with consistent Bible study. In our prayers we speak to God. In Bible study God speaks to us.

May God bless you as you go to your families and as you study the Bible with them. May He speak to your hearts. May He make us all men and women of the Word, really knowing it, and, above all, living it day by day. Let us pray.

# Prayer

"Eternal Father, we thank Thee that Thou hast called us into this covenant of study. Help us to set aside a period every day to open Thy Word and read it and listen to Thy voice speaking to us. Forgive us for the times we have neglected Thee and have loved other things rather than Thy voice speaking to us.

"Lord, I pray that Thou wilt bless each of these dear souls bowed in Thy presence. Thou knowest their needs, Thou knowest their families, Thou knowest the obstacles that are before them. Give them strength to take time to be holy. Strengthen in moments of weakness, give zeal in time of indolence, speak courage to each heart, and grant, Lord, scattered where we may be in the coming months, that we may all meet around Thy throne in the earth made new, there to see the Word Incarnate, to understand Him as He understands us, and to thank Him with immortal lips for His Great Gift.

"Take us and keep us from this day and forever in His precious name, Amen

# Selected Bibliography

Andreason, M. L. *The Sanctuary Service*. Washington: Review and Herald, 1937. 311 pp. The best book published on this subject. It does not cover of the furniture or the structure.

Danby, H. *The Mishnah*. London: Oxford University Press, 1949. 844 pp. An excellent translation of the commentary of the Jewish rabbis on the laws and services of the sanctuary.

Edersheim, A. *The Temple, its and Services as they were at the Time of Jesus Christ* London: The Religious Tract Society, n. d. 414 pp. A superb piece of research, with an excellent application of the meaning of Jewish rites to a clarification of the services of the Temple. Well worth a careful study.

Fairbairn, P. *The Typology of Scripture*. Edinburgh: T. & T. Clark, 1870. Two volumes. This classic work shows profound learning coupled with a deep devotional insight.

Gilbert, P. C. *Messiah in His Sanctuary*. Washington: Review and Herald, 1937. 248 pp. Contains much information, but has the great disadvantage of being written in question and answer form.

_____. *Practical Lessons*. Printed privately, 1914. 826 pp. A collection of material on the sanctuary and related subjects showing the bearing of Jewish customs as illustrated in the sanctuary.

Haskell, S. N. *The Cross and Its Shadow*. South Lancaster: The Bible Training School, 1914, 388 pp. A gold mine of information pleasantly written.

Jennings, D. *Jewish Antiquities*. London: W. Baynes and Son, 1825. 624 pp. This work, saturated with Hebrew lore, covers typical persons, places and times. Well worth studying.

Mather, Samuel. *The Gospel of the Old Testament*. London: Seeley and Burnside, 1834. Two volumes. These two books attempt to show how the sanctuary and its furnishings and ritual portray the gospel.

M'Ewen, W. *Grace and Truth; or the Glory and Fullness of the Redeemer Displayed: In an Attempt to Illustrate the most Remarkable Types, Figures and Allegories of the Old Testament.* London: Hamilton, Adams and Co., 1840. 382 pp. This remarkable work gives the students many insights into the meanings of the symbols of the sanctuary.

Seiss, J. A. *The Gospel in Leviticus.* Grand Rapids, Mich.: Zondervan Publishing House, n. d. 403 pp. This reprint of an old book is a good study of the laws of sacrifice.

Sleming, C. W. *These are the Garments: A Study of the Garments of the High Priest of Israel.* London: Marshal, Morgan & Scott, n. d. 128 pp. A simple and devotional study of the robes of the high priest.

Soltau, H. W. *Exposition of the, the Priestly Garments and the Priesthood.* London: Morgan and Scott, n. d. 475 pp.

_____. *The Holy Vessel and Furniture of the Tabernacle of Israel on a Uniform Scale.* London: Samuel Bagster and Sons, 1850. 66 pp.

White, Frank H. *Christ in the Tabernacle.* London: S. W. Partridge and Co., 1873. 158 pp. As its title indicates this book is a fine study of the bearing of the sanctuary upon the ministry of Jesus.

Whitfield, F. *The Tabernacle, Priesthood and Offerings of Israel.* London: Seeley, Jackson and Halliday, 1875. 372 pp. The best volume of the topic that the student has to read.

(The Author does not wholly agree with each author listed above. Each idea must be compared with the Bible.)

# Other books by TEACH Services, Inc.

**Absolutely Vegetarian**  *Lorine Tadej* . . . . . . . . . . . . . . . . . . . . . . . $ 8.95
A complete guide to maintaining a strict vegetarian lifestyle. A way to
reach your ideal weight and maintain it, as long as you live.

**The Celtic Church in Britain**  *Leslie Hardinge* . . . . . . . . . . . . . . . $ 8.95
This is an authoritative study of the beliefs and practice of the Celtic
Church which at the same time holds much interest for the non-specialist,
containing as it does fascinating descriptions of the life of the early Celtic
Christians in their monastic walled villages modelled on the Old Testa-
ment cities of refuge. Their elaborate penitential discipline was based on
Old Testament compensatory regulations. Obedience to the Scriptures
led them to establish a remarkable theocracy based on the laws of the
Pentateuch and including the keeping of the Seventh-day Sabbath.

**Don't Drink Your Milk**  *Frank Oski, MD* . . . . . . . . . . . . . . . . . . $ 7.95
Dr. Oski, the head of Pediatrics at Johns Hopkins University School of
Medicine, gives the frightening new medical facts about the world's most
overrated nutrient.

**Dove of Gold**  *Leslie Hardinge* . . . . . . . . . . . . . . . . . . . . . . . . . . . $ 7.95
This book approaches the vast subject of the Holy Spirit viewing His
functions through illustrations He himself has selected as vehicles for the
revelation of His character and work. As one observes the related aspects
of the nature and function of the natural object used as a symbol, the work
of the Holy Spirit will become clearer, and His disposition of concern
and affection much more appealing.

**Earthly Life of Jesus**  *Ken LeBrun* . . . . . . . . . . . . . . . . . . . . . . . . $19.95
Biblical accounts of each event in Christ's earthly life carefully arranged
together from the KJV Bible. Words of Jesus in red with full index.

**Garlic—Nature's Perfect Prescription**  *C. Gary Hullquist, M.D.* $ 9.95
Garlic, the Lily of Legend, has today become the focus of modern
medical research. Recognized for thousands of years for its amazing
curative powers, this bulb is today not only known for its potent bouquet
but is drawing the attention of the scientific world as a potential antibiotic,
anticancer, antioxidant, anti-aging, anti-inflammatory...the lost goes on
and on.

**Healthful Living**  *Ellen G. White* . . . . . . . . . . . . . . . . . . . . . . . . . $10.95
Wherever this book has been received, it has been recognized as a
veritable storehouse of seed thoughts relating to the great practical
themes with which it deals. Facsimile Reprint.

**Helps to Bible Study**  *J. L. Shuler* . . . . . . . . . . . . . . . . . . . . . . . . $ 2.95
A Bible marking system which contains Bible studies covering twenty-
eight topics including "The Second Coming," "The Seal of the Living
God," "Bible Temperance," and "Christian in Dress." It is simple and
practical in its approach, and will benefit all ages.

**The Illuminati 666**  *William Josiah Sutton* . . . . . . . . . . . . . . . . . $ 8.95
Find out about the Illuminati, its startling history, and how powerful it
has become. Includes a study of the origins of false religions, and the
forms they are taking today. Introduction by Roy Allan Anderson, D.D.

**In Heavenly Places Now!**  *Richard Parent* . . . . . . . . . . . . . . . . . $ 5.95
A devotional study of the sanctuary service which seeks to focus our
attention on our High Priest, Jesus Christ, who ever lives to make
intercession for us.

**The Justified Walk**  *Frank Phillips* . . . . . . . . . . . . . . . . . . . . . . . $ 8.95
Before you can rightly tackle a problem, you must first be able to clearly
understand its nature. Before you can discuss it with others, you must
first define your terms. In this book Elder Phillips makes clear how the
plan of salvation works in our daily lives. Faith, Grace, Sin, Justification,
Sanctification and Righteousness are made real and tangible.

**Lessons On Faith**  *Jones & Waggoner* . . . . . . . . . . . . . . . . . . . . . $ 6.95
This is a compilation of articles and sermons given in the 1890's by Jones
and Waggoner on Righteousness By Faith.

**Mystical Medicine**  *Warren Peters* . . . . . . . . . . . . . . . . . . . . . . . $ 7.95
Many people today have come to believe that our modern, technological
system of health care in the Western world isn't proving to be the great
boon that it was once thought to be. Frustrated and disillusioned people
are turning to "more natural" methods of treatment. As we become aware
of the intimate connection between the physical, mental and spiritual
aspects of our nature, we are flocking to holistic medicine by the
thousands.

**Living Fountains or Broken Cisterns**  *E. A. Sutherland* . . . . . . . $12.95
This book tells how we should set up our education systems to follow
the heavenly blueprint. The goal is to have the best Christian schools in
the world.

**Pioneer Stories**  *Arthur W. Spalding* . . . . . . . . . . . . . . . . . . . . . $ 9.95
It is good for children to know what their fathers and mothers did; for
sometimes that makes a pattern of what the children should do. Especially
is this true if the children are set to finish the work their parents began.
And that is the reason why this book is written, to tell the children of the
pioneers in the second advent movement the beginnings of that movement, and reasons why they are to carry it on.

**Power of Prayer**  *E. G. White* . . . . . . . . . . . . . . . . . . . . . . . . . . . $ 7.95
Prayer is our connection with God—our strength, our bridge to heaven!
As we pray, the Holy Spirit Himself unites in our petitions and "maketh
intercession for us." We are not alone in our battle of life; all heaven is
on our side!

**Preparation For Translation**  *Milton Crane* . . . . . . . . . . . . . . . . $ 7.95
This book is about YOUR preparation for translation. It is about YOUR
plans to live without a mediator after probation closes. It is about God's
plans for YOUR overcoming temptation NOW in anticipation of those
events. It is about His plans for the renewing of YOUR mind through the
final atonement ministry of Jesus. Spanish editions—$8.95.

**Quick-n-Easy Natural Recipes**  *Lorrie Knutsen* . . . . . . . . . . . . . $ 2.95
Every recipe has five or fewer ingredients and most take only minutes to
prepare. Now you can enjoy simple, natural recipes without the drudgery!

**Raw Food Treatment of Cancer**  *Kristine Nolfi* . . . . . . . . . . . . . $ 3.95
This book tells of the importance of raw vegetables in the diet of healing
and general good health. Dr. Nolfi was a physician in Denmark for over
50 years.

**Rome's Challenge**  *Catholic Mirror* . . . . . . . . . . . . . . . . . . . . . . . $  .99
"The pages of this brochure unfold to the reader one of the most glaringly
conceivable contradictions existing between the practice and theory of
the Protestant world, and unsusceptible of any rational solution, the
theory claiming the Bible alone as the teacher.

**The Sabbath**  *M. L. Andreasen* . . . . . . . . . . . . . . . . . . . . . . . . . . $ 9.95
Attacks upon the Sabbath throughout the ages have been numerous and
persistent, and they have all been grounded upon human reasoning as as
against the command of God. Men can see no reason why any other day
than one commanded by God is not just as good. Men cannot see why
one day in seven is not just as good as the seventh day. The answer, of
course, is that the difference lies in God's command. It is at this point
that man's reason sets aside a positive command of God. It is not merely
a question of this or that day, but the greater question of obedience to
God's command.

**Story of Daniel the Prophet**  *S. N. Haskell* . . . . . . . . . . . . . . . . . . $11.95
This book especially applicable to our day: points out the immediate
future and in its simplicity will attract many who might not be inclined
to read deep, argumentative works. Facsimile Reprint.

**Story of the Seer of Patmos**  *S. N. Haskell* . . . . . . . . . . . . . . . . . . $12.95
The Book of Revelation pronounces a blessing upon everyone who reads
it or hears it. Facsimile Reprint.

**Truth Triumphant**  *B. G. Wilkinson* . . . . . . . . . . . . . . . . . . . . . . . $12.95
The history of God's true Church from Ireland, to the Waldenses, the
struggle to preserve the Bible and the pure doctrine of the apostles is
disclosed. Facsimile Reprint.

### To order any of the above titles, see your local bookstore.

However, if you are unable to locate any title,
call 518/358-3652.